The Tragedies of King David

ISRAEL DRAZIN

The Tragedies
OF
King David

A close examination of the Biblical verses

gefen
publishing house
JERUSALEM • NEW YORK
Est. 1981

Cover design: Leah Ben Avraham/ Noonim Graphics
Typesetting: Raphaël Freeman, Renana Typesetting

ISBN: 978-965-229-929-1

1 3 5 7 9 8 6 4 2

Gefen Publishing House Ltd.
6 Hatzvi Street
Jerusalem 94386, Israel
972-2-538-0247
orders@gefenpublishing.com

Gefen Books
516-593-1234
orders@gefenpublishing.com

www.gefenpublishing.com

Printed in Israel

Library of Congress Cataloging-in-Publication Data

Names: Drazin, Israel, 1935- author.
Title: The tragedies of King David / by Israel Drazin.
Description: Springfield, NJ : Gefen Books ; Jerusalem : Gefen Publishing
    House, [2017]
Identifiers: LCCN 2017039946 | ISBN 9789652299291
Subjects: LCSH: David, King of Israel. | Bible. Old Testament--Criticism,
    interpretation, etc. | Rabbinical literature--History and criticism.
Classification: LCC BS580.D3 D728 2017 | DDC 222/.4092--dc23
LC record available at https://lccn.loc.gov/2017039946

Dedicated to my wife Dina

Acknowledgments

Thanks to my wife Dina, my inspiration, and our friends Dr. Norman and Estelle Wald with whom we studied Samuel for an hour on Wednesday mornings. The chapters in this book were my contribution to our sessions. Thanks also to Darlene Jospe who edited this book and prepared the Index, Table of Contents, and the List of sources, and to Ruth Pepperman who did the final editing for Gefen.

Thirty-seven books by Israel Drazin

MAIMONIDES AND RATIONAL SERIES

The Tragedies of King David

Who Really was the Biblical David?

Who was the Biblical Samuel?

Mysteries of Judaism II, How the Rabbis and Others Changed Judaism

Mysteries of Judaism

Maimonides: Reason Above All

Maimonides and the Biblical Prophets

Maimonides: The Extraordinary Mind

A Rational Approach to Judaism and Torah Commentary

Nachmanides: An Unusual Thinker

UNUSUAL BIBLE INTERPRETATION SERIES

Five books of Moses

Joshua

Judges

Ruth, Esther, and Judith

Jonah and Amos

Hosea

SCHOLARLY TARGUM BOOKS

Targumic Studies

Targum Onkelos to Exodus

Targum Onkelos to Leviticus

Targum Onkelos to Numbers

Targum Onkelos to Deuteronomy

Contents

Preface

The purpose of this volume, as it was for *Who was the Biblical Prophet Samuel?* and *Who was the Biblical David?* is to explore what the Bible actually states about one of the great figures of history. All three books explore the biblical book Samuel. The prophet and judge Samuel, as I state in that book, has only about two hundred verses devoted to him. I showed that a close examination of these passages revealed that Samuel was markedly different than many suppose him to have been. For example, he feuded with the king he appointed. I pointed out duplicate versions of several tales, and over thirty indications that the author or editor of the book did not know about the Torah of Moses, or ignored it.

In the first book about the life of David I focused on chapter 16 when David was first introduced in the book of Samuel through chapter 31, the end of I Samuel when King Saul died. The total narration of David's life begins with chapter 16 in I Samuel, and continues in II Samuel with 24 chapters and in I Kings with two. Not all of the forty-two deal with David. For example, I Samuel 28 focuses on Saul's visit to the witch of En-dor. We see that, as with Samuel, biblical scholars identify eleven events in the book that are told in two different ways. We noted that David sometimes lies and acts cruelly. We compared David with Saul and were surprised to read what the rabbis thought, and much more.

In this book, we take a close look at David's life from the beginning of II Samuel through I Kings 2. Hoenig and Rosenberg, the former scholar the late Rabbi Dr. Sydney B. Hoenig, was my uncle, wrote the following about David in their book *A Guide to the Prophets*:[1]

> "As a national figure [for after Moses, David was the first leader to unite the tribes], David alone was able to conquer the Philistines, who were not Semites

---

1. Sidney B. Hoenig and Samuel H. Rosenberg, *A Guide to the Prophets* (Yeshiva University, 1942, reprinted several times), 37–41.

but Aegean Greeks who settled in Phoenicia. They were the ones [upon whom the Romans referred when they] gave the name Palestine to the country. Their invasion of the land contemporaneously with the Israelites was thus a severe clash of two forces seeking [control of] the land of Canaan. In truth, the Philistines had power in the land until the Israelites were able to unite formidably under David. Historically, then, David's conquest of the Philistines made them a second rate power....

"Despite this unity created by David in the land, the jealousy between North and South was not extinguished. This is evident in the internal dissensions, court intrigues and rebellions of the time, and emerged later as the great catastrophe of the division of North and South in the days of Rehoboam, David's grandson....

"The most important historic fact of the entire period, undoubtedly, is the change from a nomadic to a settled agricultural mode of life, where property becomes the basis of organization....

"David is real. But his very inconsistencies and frailties before God make him more human and more lovable – a man, a plain man destined to be traditionally the *mortal* king of Israel, the founder of the Davidic dynasty.... It was David who changed a Jebusite city into the eternal Jerusalem; and gained eternal memory for himself."

PART 1

Seven Years of Preparation to Rule the United Tribes

Who Killed Saul?

II SAMUEL 1

In my book Who was the Biblical Samuel?, where I discussed the little more than 200 passages in I Samuel that deal with the last of the judges, the prophet Samuel, I focused on many subjects including the basic plot: The Israelites were divided into tribes and individual tribes had to fight alone, sometimes with one or a few other Israelite tribes, and the people approached the aged Samuel, whom they respected, and beseeched him to appoint a king. Samuel was hurt. He had two sons whom he had appointed as judges, but the people rejected them as their leaders. He felt that despite years of service to his people, they were rebuffing him. After speaking with God who advised him to accept the people's request, he anointed Saul as Israel's first king. Samuel's resentment remained and two chapters offer two different reasons why God decided to end Saul's dynasty. Probably because of being discarded by God and Samuel, Saul became depressed and rather than taking out his anger against the prophet, his anger was displaced upon David.

In Who Really Was the Biblical David?, among much else, I showed that David may have been planning all along to succeed Saul. The Bible describes him acting with self-interest and lying to people on several occasions.

In both books, there are more than several dozen instances where people perform acts which are contrary to what the Torah demands. It is as if they had no idea that the Torah existed. They never mention the Torah. There are also almost a dozen times where some scholars feel convinced that the book contains two versions of a single story.

WHAT HAPPENS IN II SAMUEL 1?

The story of David's rise to the throne of Israel can be divided into three parts: (1) I Samuel 16–20 tells of the time that David served under King Saul, (2) I Samuel 21–31 describes events while the two are estranged, and (3) II Samuel 1–7 depicts David as king over the southern nation of Judea.

In I Samuel's final chapter, Saul led the Israelites in a defensive battle against the overwhelming force of Philistines and Israel lost. Many Israelites were killed, including Saul's son Jonathan and his brothers Abinadab and Malchishua, three of the four sons of Saul.[1] Philistine archers discovered Saul's whereabouts and began to shoot arrows at him. Although Saul was not hit,[2] he asked his armor-bearer to kill him with his sword because of fear that the Philistines would "make a mockery of me," if he would be captured alive.[3] The armor-bearer refused to kill his king, so Saul "took his sword and fell upon it." The armor-bearer saw that his king was dead and also committed suicide. And "all his men" died.[4] The Philistines found the bodies of Saul and his sons and cut off Saul's head.[5] II Samuel begins with David hearing about the death of Saul, and his reactions. We see again an act contrary to the demands of the Torah, some scholars contending that chapter one of II Samuel is another version of the death of Saul, the prior version being in the last chapter of I Samuel. In II Samuel, David is acting with self-interest, aggressively, and lying.

The story began on the third day[6] after David returned from a battle against a

---

1. Ish-bosheth is not mentioned, and we do not know why. Yehuda Kiel, *Samuel*. 2 vols. Daat Mikra. (Jerusalem: Mossad HaRav Kook, 1981) mentions three speculations: He did not join in the battle (Radak); the practice at the time was for no more than three sons to join a fight, as in 17:13 where only three sons of Jesse, brothers of David, joined Saul in that war; or he participated in the battle but was unharmed. He may have been at the battle, but fled when the war turned against the Israelites (Abarbanel).

2. According to Radak. Kiel mentions that others interpret the tale that Saul was wounded. The Bible is silent on this point.

3. Rabbi Dr. S. Goldman, *Samuel*. (London: The Soncino Press, 1951) adds the idea about the mockery being made while Saul is alive.

4. Verse 5, "all" is hyperbole.

5. Arnold B. Ehrlich, *Mikra Kipheshuto* [The Bible according to its literal meaning]. Ed. Harry M. Orlinsky (New York: Ktav Publishing House, 1969) notes that it seems to have been a practice among the ancients to decapitate the great of other nations, as David did to Goliath in I Samuel 17.

6. The number three appears frequently in the Bible, as will be commented upon later in this chapter.

large group of Amalekites who had attacked his camp and taken hostages while David was absent. David agreed in the end of I Samuel to help Saul's army in the fight against the Philistines, whether deceptively or otherwise, the Bible is obscure on this point, but some of the Philistine leaders refused his aid in their war against Israel, and David returned to his encampment to find that it had been attacked. David was victorious in this battle against Amalek.

David was approached by a man who told him that the Israelites lost the battle with the Philistines and there were many Israelite deaths including those of Saul and his son Jonathan. He was an Amalekite. "Externally, the young man has the usual signs of the mourner, clothes rent and earth upon his head."[7] He claimed he escaped from the Israelite camp, that he found Saul leaning on his spear wounded,[8] Philistine chariots and horsemen were approaching, Saul beseeched him to kill him, he saw that it was certain that Saul would die shortly from his wound, so he killed the king, took his crown and bracelet,[9] and brought them to David.

---

7. Hans Wilhelm Hertzberg, *I & II Samuel* (The Old Testament Library. The Westminster Press, 1964), 236. He adds, "But his purpose is, in fact, to bring to Saul's enemy a message which promises a reward." Samuel Abramski, ed., *Samuel*, Olam Hatanakh (Jerusalem: Divrei Hayamim, 2002), suggests that it is possible that the Amalekite took a dual approach: He dressed as a mourner to show his distress over the death of Saul and David's friend, Saul's son Jonathan in case David was not sad over their death, but at the same time hoped that bringing the news of their death would result in David rewarding him. Olam Hatanakh, Kiel, and others add that the behavior of the Amalekite shows that the idea that David would succeed Saul as king was accepted by a large number of Israelites. P. Kyle McCarter, Jr., *II Samuel*, The Anchor Bible (New York: Doubleday, 1984), notes that the story of the Amalekite informing David of the catastrophic defeat in the war against the Philistines and the death of sons is similar to the messenger's report to Eli of the Philistine victory at Ebenezer in I Samuel 4:12–17, and the Amalekites torn clothes and disheveled condition reminds us of the ruse of the Gibeonites in Joshua 9:3–15, and the description of the Amalekite as a *naar* may suggest that he was a soldier since the word is sometimes used to describe a military man.

8. I Samuel 31 states that Saul fell upon his sword. In an attempt to reconcile this chapter with 31. Isaac Abarbanel, *Perush Abarbanel* (New York: Seforim Torah Vodaath, 1955) and Levi ben Gershon (Gersonides), *Peirushei Ralbag Nevi'im Rishonim* (Jerusalem: Mossad Harav Kook, 2008), state that although the text has "spear" it refers to the king's sword.

9. While the consensus interpretation is that the Amalekite brought the crown and bracelet to show them to David because the two items were part of Saul's royal regalia, II Kings 11:12 indicates that they are insignia of royalty. However, ibn Caspi, quoted by Kiel, supposes that Saul's bracelet was *tefillin*.

David and his band tore their clothes, wept, and fasted until evening as a sign of mourning for all Israelites who had fallen in the battle.[10]

David questioned the Amalekite,[11] either immediately, as Ehrlich supposes, or after the mourning acts, for as usual, Scripture is unclear. He ordered one of his soldiers to kill the Amalekite.[12] David said, "Your blood is upon your own head: for your mouth testified against you when you said, 'I have slain the Lord's anointed.'"[13]

DAVID LAMENTED

David then recited a dirge that lacked any religious feeling in which the refrain "how are the mighty fallen" is repeated three times, a second appearance of three in the chapter.[14] He addressed the lament to the people of Judah and not all of Israel because David was not yet the ruler of the northern tribes.[15] Hertzberg writes: "There is no reason for doubting David's authorship of the lament. In 1 Samuel 16:18, he is celebrated not only for his musical ability, but also for his power of expression." He adds that the lament is a "masterful song in which David has raised a memorial not only for Saul and Jonathan but also for himself."[16]

---

10. The rabbis in the Babylonian Talmud, *Mo'ed Katan* 26a derive from David's act that it is obligatory for Jews to rend their garments upon the death of a prince as a sign of mourning (Kiel, Goldman, and others).

11. Ehrlich, *Mikra Kipheshuto*, notes that not only didn't the Israelites obey the Torah command to exterminate Amalek, they allowed the Amalekites to live in Canaan with them. Radak opines that the Amalekite was a sincere convert to Judaism.

12. Radak suggests that the Amalekite did not reveal that he was from the enemy tribe Amalek; but one of David's soldiers identified him. The messenger did not want to reveal he was an Amalekite; he remembered that Saul fought against his people and was concerned that David also disliked them. (Radak bases this understanding upon the wording of verse 8, which literally states "and it was said."

13. See Israel Drazin, *Who Really Was the Biblical David?* (Jerusalem: Gefen Publishing House, 2017), chapters 24 and 26, when he spared Saul's life, David was concerned that when he became king he might be killed. He strongly opposed regicide, as seen again in 11 Samuel 4:10ff. While the Babylonian Talmud *Baba Metziah* 3b states "an admission by a defendant is equal to a hundred witnesses," this rule only applies to monetary, not capital cases. Thus, as will be discussed below, David's act was contrary to later rabbinical law.

14. Verses 19, 25, and 27.

15. A careful reading of Saul's life shows he did not rule over Judah. Some Septuagint versions have "Israel" and one has "Israel and Judah."

16. Hertzberg, *1 & 11 Samuel*, 238.

Verse 18 states that David's lament "is written in the book of Jashar. This book is mentioned only here and in Joshua 10:13 where Joshua celebrated his victory.[17] It is one of many ancient books which are lost. We do not know what it contains besides beside the two songs.[18]

TWO VERSIONS OF TRADITIONS IN THE BIBLE

Many scholars insist that there are a large number of dual-versions in the Hebrew Bible. They contend that whoever edited the Bible assembled divergent accounts of events, some in manuscripts, some oral traditions, considered each either significant or holy, did not decide which is correct, and placed each in the text despite one contradicting the other. They cite Genesis 1 and 2 as examples. In 1, God is called Elohim and creates, according to them, a being that is both male and female.[19] In 2, God is called *Y-h-v-h* Elohim and creates a man first and then a woman out of his side.[20] Some see Genesis 6:19, 20 and 7:2 as two divergent narratives. In the first, Noah was told by God to take only a pair of "every living thing." In chapter 7, he was instructed to take seven pairs of the "clean beasts."[21] A third example, is the description of the sale of Joseph by his brothers. It appears that two accounts are entangled. Was it Reuben who tried to save Joseph in Genesis

---

17. The Aramaic Targum, Radak, and others contend that the book of Jashar refers to the Five Books of Moses. The book is also mentioned in the Septuagint translation of 1 Kings 8:12–13.

18. Joshua's song is an obvious hyperbole, as are all other songs in scripture, including Moses's song praising God for saving the Israelites at the Red Sea. In both instances the prose narrative is realistic and lacks the "miracle" in the song. Realizing that all biblical songs are exaggerations should prompt readers to read the song carefully and not think, for example, that David's statement about Jonathan in the song "Your love was wonderful to me, more than the love of women," refers to homosexuality. On this later point, Ehrlich comments that by comparing his love of Jonathan to his love of women, David is revealing how passionate he is about women, and it is because of this passion that he later acts improperly with Bat-sheba. In contrast, Radak understands "women" to refer to David's two wives that he had at that time.

19. This interpretation is also in many Midrashim and may have been derived from the Greek philosopher Plato's *Symposium* where Aristophanes states that humans were originally a single being which was both male and female. After being separated each part yearns to rejoin the other half.

20. Some translate the Hebrew word as "rib." Arguably this is not a dual version. Scripture very frequently makes a general statement (God created a man and a woman) and then later gives the details (first man, then woman).

21. This may also not be a doublet. The "seven pair" exception is simply mentioned later. The Bible frequently adds details when it delves more deeply or repeats a tale.

37:21–36 or Judah, was Joseph sold to Ishmaelites or Midianites? In my prior book *Who Really Was the Biblical David?* I described about a dozen instances where some scholars identified a dual version of an event. For example, I Samuel 16 described Saul meeting David when Saul needed a musician to sooth his depression and David was called a warrior at that time, Saul loved him, and requested of David's father that he be able to remain with Saul. In contrast, chapter 17 described David as a shepherd with no warrior experience who Saul did not know when he asked the king for permission to fight Goliath.

The Interpreter's Bible, Ehrlich, and others consider II Samuel 1 as a second version of how Saul died. In I Samuel he dies, but in II Samuel the Amalekite claims he found Saul alive and killed him.

Radak and Gersonides contend that it is possible that the Amalekite's claim is true: the wound Saul suffered when he fell on his sword did not kill Saul and the armor bearer was mistaken when he thought that Saul was dead.

Smith writes:[22] "The easiest hypothesis is that the Amalekite fabricated his story. But the whole narrative is against this. David has no inkling that the man is not truthful, nor does the author suggest it."

Goldman notes that some modern scholars posit that the events in chapter 31 are true and the allegation by the Amalekite was a fabrication. The Amalekite may have been a camp follower who plundered the belongings of the fallen soldiers. He may have discovered Saul's body and his property and brought it to David, whom he had heard had many difficulties with Saul, and hoped to receive a reward for killing David's enemy.

TIT FOR TAT

The idea developed in many cultures that a person is punished for his misdeed in the same way that he committed the misdeed. Slap someone and you will be slapped. Insult another and you will be insulted. In English, the notion is called "tit for tat." In Hebrew it is *midah keneged midah*, "measure for measure." It is discussed in the Babylonian Talmud.[23] Many call the notion superstition: it

---

22. H.P. Smith, *A Critical and Exegetical Commentary on the Book of Samuel*, International Critical Commentary (Edinburgh: Clark, 1899), cited by P. Kyle McCarter, Jr.
23. *Sota* 8b, 9a; *Megilah* 12b; and *Sanhedrin* 90a, b, and 100a, b.

rarely happens, and when it does it is simply happenstance. Some insist that the punishment is inflicted by God. Others that it is part of nature. People can cite many examples of it, such as the life and death of Saul. While not mentioning *midah keneged midah,* Ehrlich supposes that the author of Samuel inserted the story of the Amalekite killing Saul to highlight how much God hated Saul: Saul failed to carry out the divine command in 1 Samuel 15 to destroy Amalek and he did not do so. Samuel stated there that as a punishment his dynasty would cease with his death. 11 Samuel 1, according to Ehrlich, rebuked and humiliated Saul further by stating he was killed by an Amalekite.[24]

A POSSIBLE THIRD TRADITION OF SAUL'S DEATH

The Interpreter's Bible, Segal, and others also see a discrepancy between 11 Samuel 1 and 11 Samuel 4. In the first the Amalekite claimed he killed Saul and David ordered his followers to execute him. In the second, "David describes the Amalekite simply reporting the death of Saul, and that he himself killed the man with his own hands."[25] *The Interpreter's Bible* is convinced the Amalekite's story is true and this is a duplicate tradition, while Segal feels certain that neither the author of Samuel nor David thought the Amalekite was anything other than a liar seeking a reward from David.[26] The only item that David believed was that the Israelites lost the war and Saul and his family were killed. Segal refers readers to 1 Chronicles 10 where the author only mentions the chapter 31 true version and not the Amalekite's claim.

All of these apparently variant sources can be explained as non-duplications. For example, in regard to the difference between 1 Samuel 31 and 11 Samuel 1, some commentators see the Amalekite's claim in chapter 31 that he murdered the king as a lie told in the hope of gaining an award. 11 Samuel 4 can be understood as a brief summary and when David remarked he killed him, he meant he ordered the man killed.

---

24. Ehrlich, *Mikra Kipheshuto,* imagines that chapter 31, which does not humiliate Saul, was composed by a scribe friendly to Saul, while chapter 1 was composed by a friend of David.
25. George A. Buttrick, *The Interpreter's Bible* (New York: Abingdon, 1957), 1041, is incorrect. The words "with his own hands" is not in the text.
26. M.T. Segal, *Mevo Hamikra* (Introduction to the Bible; Jerusalem: Kiryat Sefer, 1977).

EXECUTION WITHOUT A TRIAL

There are many instances in Scripture where biblical figures, including prophets, perform acts that are clearly contrary to the Five Books of Moses, as the rabbis interpret the biblical laws. One could argue that the people acted as they did because they did not know about the existence of the Torah. And the Torah did not exist before the time of Judean King Josiah in the seventh century BCE. The rabbis dismiss this idea and generally explain that in each such instance the circumstances of the time required the people to act as they did. They called this *horaat shaah,* which can be defined as "a decision under an emergency," "a temporary decision," or "a special dispensation." It can be contrasted with *horaat ledorot,* "a permanent decision" or "a permanent law." Thus, Gersonides comments on this chapter that David was allowed to kill the Amalekite without a trial, and without the witnesses, and to use the man's confession, which are not allowed under the rabbinical interpretation of scripture, because of *horaat shaah*: it was necessary to teach the people that regicide is wrong. Maimonides[27] writes that a king may ignore the rules of due process to "set right the moral climate of society according to the needs of the time."[28]

The Babylonian Talmud *Baba Kama* 92a addresses the question: why was the man guilty of murder when he was commanded by a king to do the act [to kill him]? The Talmud explains that one is forbidden to kill oneself, to request others to kill him or her, and the person who kills another under these conditions is guilty of murder.

Ehrlich ignores the issue and argues that David executed the man who claimed to have killed the king to prompt Israel to realize that he had no hand in the death of Saul, he had positive feelings about him, and anyone who thinks that regicide is proper will be killed. In short, he acted with self-interest.

THE NUMBER THREE

The ubiquitous number three appears twice in this chapter, once to tell how many days it took David and his troops to return from the Philistine battlefield to Ziklag and once to tell us that the slave David found who informed him where

---

27. *Mishneh Torah, Sanhedrin* 18:6 and *Hilkhot Malakhim* 3:10.
28. *Horaat shaah* is discussed in more detail in the Excursus.

the marauders were located hadn't eaten or drunk for three days. The number is used frequently also in other cultures and even in fairy tales.[29] *A New Concordance of the Old Testament* shows that it appears in the Hebrew Bible 736 times.[30]

Ibn Ezra interpreted the oft-occurring number seven as a symbol of completeness.[31] Three, on the other hand, is "always bad because it is half" (or, more precisely, close to half) of seven. It is the turning point to the change that will reach its climax with seven. Thus, in Genesis 34:25, the people of Shechem were sickest on the third day after their circumcision. The idea of seven signifying completeness is also the view of other writers, such as S.R. Hirsch.[32] Hirsch felt that eight signified the beginning of something new. He writes elsewhere that this is why Judaism requires male children to be circumcised on the eighth day because with the circumcision the child enters the Jewish community.

Baruch Epstein agrees as well. He states that everything becomes complete with seven.[33] Thus, a person naturally only feels full joy after a seven-day celebration, as in the seven days of a wedding celebration and the seven days of Passover and Sukkot. Similarly, he felt that mourning can only be complete and cathartic if a person has seven days of strict mourning, called *shiva*.

Thus, it is possible that the word *sheva*, "seven," is related to *sova*. The latter means satisfaction and completeness, as in eating until a person is satisfied. An example is 1 Chronicles 23:1, which states that David "was old and *sova* in days."

Joseph ibn Caspi, as the Greek philosopher Aristotle before him, did not consider the number seven as a complete number but as a metaphor for "many." Aristotle had written that three (and not seven) is a symbol of completeness since

---

29. Today, many superstitious Jews spit three times to ward off the evil eye when confronted with an unwanted occurrence. Many people in many cultures considered three a magic number; it was believed that if a person asked for something three times it would occur.

30. Abraham Even-Shoshan, ed. *A New Concordance of the Old Testament* (Kiryat-Sefer, 1989).

31. Commentaries to Exodus 3:15; Leviticus 22:27, 23:24, 26:18; Numbers 23:1; and Deuteronomy 28:7. See Israel Drazin, *Maimonides and the Biblical Prophets* (Jerusalem: Gefen Publishing House, 2009), chapter 39, for the use of seven in over a hundred instances in Judaism and dozens in other cultures.

32. S.R. Hirsch, *The Pentateuch* (New York: Judaica Press, 1971). Commentary to Leviticus 12:2, 3.

33. Baruch Epstein, *Tosaphot Berakhah* (Moreshet Publishing House, 1999), book one, 87–89, and *Mekor Barukh* (Lithuania, Rom, 1928), part 3, chapter 26.

it has a beginning, middle, and end. Caspi explains that Noah did not literally take seven clean animals into his ark, but the number seven indicates that he took many of them.[34]

34. B. Herring, *Caspi's Gevia Kesef* (Ktav Publishing House, 1982), 158. Caspi's name is also spelt Kaspi.

Excursus: When Can the Torah Law Be Ignored?

The rule of "extraordinary needs of the time" means, in essence, that sometimes a situation is so extraordinary that unusual steps must be taken to save Judaism or the Jewish people. The rule is mentioned in several midrashic and talmudic sources.[35]

---

35. *Midrash Sifrei Deuteronomy* 175 and the Babylonian Talmud, *Yevamot* 90b, allow a prophet to act contrary to Torah law when the "extraordinary needs of the time" require it. Commenting upon Deuteronomy 18:15, which requires people to obey prophets, the Midrash and the Talmud state that one must listen to the prophet "even if he directs you to violate one of the commands recorded in the Torah – just as Elijah on Mount Carmel [in 1 Kings 18] – obey him in every respect in accordance with the needs of the hour (*lefi shaah*)." Elijah brought sacrifices outside the prescribed area, a prohibited act that was punishable by death, but it was permissible in this instance *lefi shaah*, for it was necessary to disprove the prophets of Baal and show the people that God is the true deity.

Sanhedrin 46a contains another example. It states: "Rabbi Eliezer ben Jacob said, 'I heard that the court may [when necessary] impose flagellation and pronounce [capital] sentences even when they are not [warranted] by the Torah. This is not done to disregard the Torah, but in order to make a fence around it [i.e., safeguard it]. It once happened that a man rode on the Sabbath during the Greek era. He was brought before the court and stoned. It was not because he was liable [by law] to this penalty. It was done because of *hashaah tzrikhah* [it was required by the circumstances of the time]. It also happened that a man had intercourse with his wife [in public] under a fig tree. He was brought to the court and flogged. This was also not done because he merited it. Rather it was required by the circumstances of the time.'"

Maimonides addresses the issue of *lefi shaah* and *horaat shaah* and *hashaah tzrikhah*, all terms expressing the same idea, in several places. In his *Mishneh Torah, Hilkhot Yesodei Hatorah* 9:3, for example, he writes about prophets and repeats the law contained in the Midrash and Talmuds, but, as we will see, he extends the exemption, and states that it applies not only to a prophet, but also to a Jewish court: "When a prophet...tells us to violate one or many of the Torah *mitzvot*...it is a *mitzva* to listen to him. We learned this from the early sages, who had it as a part of oral law...we must accept his [the prophet's] decree in all things except idol worship according to the needs of the hour [*lefi shaah*]. For example, Elijah [in 1 Kings 18] sacrificed on Mount Carmel, outside the Temple premises."

SOME OF MANY BIBLICAL EXAMPLES OF THIS RULE

1. Moses killed the Israelites who worshipped the golden calf in Exodus 32:27 even though capital punishment is only authorized when culprits are warned ahead of time that the contemplated act is wrong and that its punishment is death, which did not occur. Rabbis argue that the punishment was necessary in this instance to inform the people of the gravity of the offense.

2. Moses instructed his brother Aaron's sons, the newly installed priests, not to cut their hair or cut their garments as a sign of mourning in Leviticus 10:6 even though the law allows these acts of mourning. Rabbis say it was necessary so that the first day of their priesthood should not be marred by solemn acts of mourning.

3. The tribal leaders brought sacrifices in Numbers 7:14 that were contrary to law: among other things, individuals are not allowed to bring incense offerings and the freewill sacrifices were offered on the Sabbath. Rabbis state that since this

---

In his *Perush Hamishnah* to *Sanhedrin* 6:2, and in his *Mishneh Torah, Hilkhot Sanhedrin* 18:6, Maimonides clarifies that the execution of Achan was by the authority of *horaat shaah* since Jewish law does not inflict capital punishment upon a person who confesses theft or based on the testimony of a prophet who had a vision that the defendant committed the crime.

In his *Mishneh Torah, Hilkhot Mamrim* 2:4, Maimonides indicates that the power derived from Deuteronomy 18:15 was extended to a court. It may abolish a biblical law temporarily, but only as a *horaat shaah* (a ruling to meet the unusual needs of the hour). If the court sees that it is necessary to strengthen Judaism by rendering corporal or capital punishment that is not sanctioned by the Torah, it may do so, but only as a temporary measure to bring many people back to Judaism. This, he continues, resembles a situation in which a doctor may see that it is necessary to amputate an arm or a leg in order to save a person's life. This, he concludes, is like the rule in the Babylonian Talmud, *Yoma* 85b: one should desecrate a single Sabbath to save a person's life and make it possible for him to observe many Sabbaths.

He mentions this judicial power also in his *Hilkhot Sanhedrin* 24:4, and gives three examples of the application of *horaat shaah*. He states that although the law requires that a court may only render capital punishment under certain circumstances, including warning the potential violator not to perform the act, clear testimony by witnesses, and close scrutiny of the witnesses, this was not done during the period when many Jews began to follow the Greek practices. Thus a person who cohabited with his wife publicly and another who rode a horse on the Sabbath were killed by the court under the rule of *horaat shaah* to impress upon the people that these acts were not permissible. Similarly, the religious leader Shimon ben Shetach killed eighty witches in a single day, as indicated in *Mishnah Sanhedrin* 6:4, even though women are not killed in this manner and a court may not kill more than a single person in a single day. It was necessary because the notion of witchcraft was drawing the masses away from proper Jewish thought.

was the first day of the consecration of the sanctuary, these sacrificial offerings were necessary.

4. The person who cursed God in Leviticus 24:12 was executed, even though he was not warned, in order to highlight the significance of this outrageous misdeed.

5. Some rabbis argue that Samson was granted an exception and allowed to marry a Philistine woman in Judges 14 because of a special need: he required an excuse to attack the Philistines who later took advantage of his wife.

THE URGENCY IN SOME OF THE EXAMPLES CITED BY THE RABBIS IS DIFFICULT TO FIND

1. Contrary to the accepted law, the tribe of Levi was given one fiftieth of the spoils of the war against Midian in Numbers 31:20.

2. Joshua, according to the understanding of the story in the Babylonian Talmud, *Megilah* 14b, was able to marry the Canaanite *zona* ("prostitute" or "innkeeper") Rahab, despite the Israelites being commanded not to marry Canaanites and to kill them.

3. In Joshua 6, Joshua engaged in a preemptive battle against Jericho on the seventh day of the Israelites' march around the city, which according to some rabbis was the Sabbath.

4. Joshua executed Achan in Joshua 7 for theft without a trial and with no witnesses of the act.

5. Some people who insist that women cannot be judges explain that Deborah was an exception (Judges 4 and 5) because of the exigency of the time.

6. In II Samuel 1:15, David executed a man from Amalek who admitted that he killed King Saul, even though the rabbis understood that a confession could not be used for proof of a misdeed and as grounds for execution.[36]

7. Joshua brought sacrifices on Mount Ebal in Joshua 8:30.

8. Gideon sacrificed away from the Tabernacle in Judges 6:25, 26 and committed about a half a dozen other violations.

9. Manoah also brought a sacrifice outside of the prescribed area in Judges 3:19.

10. Similarly, in I Samuel 7:9, the prophet Samuel offered a sacrifice outside the prescribed area and committed several other violations.

---

36. Aaron Kirschenbaum, *Self-Incrimination in Jewish Law* (New York: Burning Bush Press, 1970).

11. The inhabitants of Bet Shemesh deviated even more. In 1 Samuel 6:15, they sacrificed the Philistine oxen that carried the ark that had been captured by the Philistines back to the Israelite camp. According to Rabbi Eliezer in the Babylonian Talmud, *Avoda Zarah* 24b, one is prohibited from sacrificing non-Israelite oxen.

PROBLEMS WITH THE SOLUTION OF *HORAAT SHAAH*

The subject of *horaat shaah* is complex and raises many questions. We will examine a few.

1. Could a modern Orthodox court justify killing Reform Jews with the concept of *horaat shaah*? Could they claim that they are defending the faith? Wouldn't this be seen as fanaticism?
2. Is it possible that the rabbis invented the concept of *horaat shaah* to explain why the biblical leaders acted contrary to the rabbis' post-biblical interpretation of the law?
3. If the concept of *horaat shaah* existed in the biblical era and the biblical personalities knew that their acts were violations of biblical law and were allowed only because of the exigencies of the time to teach some lesson or accomplish some unusual deed, why doesn't the Torah mention this authority and the lesson derived from the act? Why does it leave the Torah readers with the idea that the biblical characters acted improperly?
4. Again, assuming that the biblical leaders acted contrary to Torah law, why did they have to take such extreme measures? Couldn't the lesson that Joshua wanted to teach be taught without killing Achan? Was it necessary to execute his family? What was accomplished by stoning and burning his animals?

YEHEZKEL KAUFMANN'S EXPLANATION

Yehezkel Kaufmann explains that Joshua was very careful not to allow the Israelites to settle on land during the entire period they were conquering Canaan.[37] "The Canaanites had a most important technical-military advantage: they had a trained army with cavalry and chariots. The Israelite army consisted of popular levies, an

---

37. Yehezkel Kaufmann, *A Biblical Account of the Conquest of Canaan* (Jerusalem: The Hebrew University Magnes Press, 1985), 138–145.

army of sword-bearing infantry. But the Israelites were disunited.... The tribes of Israel could conquer them only by unity." Thus Joshua had to keep them together and keep them united under his leadership. This explains why he kept them in the Gilgal camp during all the years of the conquest of Canaan – according to tradition, seven years – and why he could not allow them to establish homes and settle. If they settled, they would not return to fight. "This would appear to be the hidden reason for the banning and cursing of Jericho.... He has to separate the war from the settling."

This also explains the execution of Achan and his family. It was "a most grimly impressive ceremony. The harsh punishment was essential to reinforce that absolute submission to the prophetic leader [Joshua] without which [submission and unity] there was no hope of victory. Moreover, the discovery of the sinner and his punishment dispelled the terror by defeat. Indeed, the confidence, that God's hand was to be seen in everything that happened, was now strengthened."

Could we develop similar reasons for the other examples of *horaat shaah*?

ANOTHER SOLUTION

There is a simpler and more understandable solution. Laws develop over time; it is therefore reasonable to assume that the examples that the rabbis cited of apparent violations were acts that the perpetrators felt were not contrary to law. These laws simply did not exist during their lifetime; they were post-biblical rabbinical enactments.

Civil War

II SAMUEL 2

After learning that Saul was dead, David enquired of the Lord whether he should go from his encampment to Judea. Scripture does not reveal the reason for his trip, but we can imagine that he was thinking that he had now been handed the opportunity to be king of Judah.[38] God replied that he should go to Hebron, which we can understand literally as a divine communication or as an internal decision by David, his belief that he would be better able to fulfil his goal there, and he was right. As Goldman writes: "David was now the only man in Israel who had both connected with the royal household and endowed with the political experience, the military genius, the personal brilliance, and the public esteem to undertake with success the slow and arduous task of rebuilding Israel's political fortunes."[39]

THE OBSCURITY OF FIVE EVENTS

Chapter 2 describes five events: (1) David took his family and all of his troops and went to Hebron in Judah where he was anointed king of Judah. (2) David praised the citizens of Jabesh-gilead. (3) Abner, the commander of the late King Saul's army and his relative, crowned Saul's son Ish-bosheth as king of the northern nation Israel. (4) Dating the reigns of the two kings. (5) Civil war between the forces of the two kings in Gibeon. These events contain obscurities because of the customary manner in which Scripture describes events, and opinions differ on how the events should be understood.

---

38. As I mentioned in the past, I understand that even as early as the days of Joshua, the Bible is hinting that Judah stood apart from the northern tribes of Israel. Thus, at this time, David was not thinking of uniting all the tribes into a single kingdom. He knew that Saul's son was alive and would succeed him as king of Israel.
39. Goldman, *Samuel*, 192.

TRAVEL TO HEBRON

By telling us that God told David to go to Hebron where the people of Judah would anoint him king, the "narrator wants his audience to understand that David's return to Judah was intended by God."[40]

The Hebrew text is literally "cities of Hebron," which led commentators such as Segal to understand that David divided his troop among the various cities near Hebron so as not to overload one city with so many people, not to frighten the inhabitants, and to help assure that he would be protected.

David was anointed king three times: once by the prophet Samuel in I Samuel 16:13, here by Judeans, and later in II Samuel 5:3 as king of the united Israel. The first instance shows us the divine will, the second the will of Judah, and the third the will of all Israel. We do not know specifically who anointed him in this chapter. It could have been by an assembly, the leaders of Hebron, the leaders of the area, or the leaders of the towns where David sent gifts in I Samuel 30:26–31.

"David's reign in Hebron seems to have been an important stage in the development of the bonds that eventually made possible the unification of Judah and Israel under a single ruler."[41] Ehrlich adds that David acted cleverly; had he been precipitate and attempted to rule all Israel immediately, he would never have been king of Judah or Israel. By being king of Judah, David apparently also reigned over the tribe of Simeon which resided within the territory of Judah as indicated in Joshua 19:1, 9.[42]

RELATIONS WITH JABESH-GILEAD

After being crowned king of Judah, David acted to extend his rule with shrewdness and war. He informed the non-Judean city of Jabesh-gilead, which was located in Transjordan and was the principal city of Gilead, that he heard that they had rescued the bodies of Saul and his sons from the Philistines.[43] He promised them protection as a reward for their deed, possibly hoping to extend his influence beyond Judea.[44] Scripture does not reveal their response. However, since this

---

40. McCarter, I Samuel, 83.
41. Ibid., 89.
42. Kiel, Samuel.
43. I Samuel 31:11ff.
44. His strategy seems to have failed and Jabesh-gilead seems to have remained faithful to Ish-bosheth, Saul's son.

attempt was followed by Ish-bosheth settling in Gilead, it seems clear that this first attempt by David to extend his kingdom failed (Segal, Olam Hatanakh, and others). Ehrlich asks why the brief tale is mentioned and replies that it shows David's initial attempt to charm the various parts of Israel with words and how, despite being a brilliant poet, he fails and needs to move forward with acts.

THE CROWNING OF ISH-BOSHETH

Saul's son Ish-bosheth, formally called Ish-baal,[45] was crowned king of Israel by Saul's erstwhile commander Abner, who was the son of Saul's uncle, his first cousin. Ish-bosheth was then forty-years-old.[46] He settled in Gilead, on the eastern side of the Jordan, probably to avoid easy and disturbing constant contact, at least initially, with the Philistines and Judea. Most commentators agree that Ish-bosheth was weak and relied totally on Abner (Olam Hatanakh).

LENGTH OF THE REIGNS OF THE TWO KINGS

The chapter states that David was king of Judah for seven years and six months and Ish-bosheth was Israel's sovereign for two years. This reckoning conflicts with chapter 5 which indicates that David became king of united Israel immediately after Ish-bosheth's death. Many proposed solutions are offered. Goldman and Kiel suggest that at first Ish-bosheth was king over a smaller area and ruled over the entire northern kingdom for only two years. Radak and Tosaphot on the Babylonian Talmud *Sanhedrin* 20a propose that Ish-bosheth reigned with full power for two years but his authority diminished after that time. Rashi contends that Israel had no king for five years and Ish-bosheth was placed on Israel's throne two years before he died. Another possibility is that the number two is an error,

---

45. In 1 Chronicles 8:33 and 9:39, he is called Ish-baal. During early Israelite history, Israelites used the name Baal, which means "Lord," as a name for God, just as we use "Lord" today, and many Israelites added Baal to their names, as we add El, "God," to many names today, as in Israel and Gabriel. Thus, Ish-baal's birth name does not necessarily indicate idol worship. Around the time of King David, the use of Baal became unacceptable. The Bible mocks people who have names ending with Baal and substitutes *bosheth*, "embarrassment," as in 1 Chronicles 8:33–34; 9:36, 39–40; 14:7; II Samuel 2:2, 8, 12, 15; 4:4, 9, and more.

46. It is unlikely that Saul's son was forty years old, so since the number is a round number and is frequently used in the Bible to indicate a rather long time, Scripture may mean here that Ish-bosheth was a mature young man.

as is his age forty, because he appears to be quite young in the book with Abner taking charge.[47]

CIVIL WAR BEGINS OVER A GAME

There were apparently many wars between David's kingdom in Judah and Ish-bosheth's in Israel, but only the battle of Gibeon in chapter 3 is described in detail because of its bearing on the assassination of Abner. In chapter 2, the two generals of the two kingdoms met, Abner of the north and Joab of the south, and the two suggested a contest between their forces, twelve men from each side. We do not know why Abner's troops went south to Gibeon and David's went north to the town,[48] why twelve soldiers were selected from each army, whether the contest began as a harmless game but when possibly one man was accidentally killed the friendly contest deteriorated into a battle, or whether the contest from its very beginning was intended to be a real fight to the finish, a battle by representatives, an ancient practice, with God deciding who would win.[49] We also do not know what part, if any, David played in the episode. All twenty-four men were killed. A battle of both armies followed with David's forces winning.

Abner fled and was pursued by Joab's brother Asahel. Abner was reluctant to fight Asahel and precipitate a blood feud, but Asahel would not let up. Abner suggested that he turn to the right or left, take one of the soldiers, and take his weapon.[50] Asahel refused, so Abner hit him with the end of his spear, perhaps not intending to kill him (Radak, Hertzberg, Ehrlich, and others), but Asahel died. Ehrlich adds: Scripture relates that Abner had no intention to kill Joab's

---

47. The statement that Ish-bosheth ruled for only two years parallels the error that Saul was king for only two years in I Samuel 13:1.

48. McCarter suggests that Abner's expedition was probably provoked by David's overture to Jabesh-gilead. Abner may have rightly assumed that this was a clear challenge to Ish-bosheth's authority. Segal and Kiel propose that Abner went south to assure that the Gibeonites would remain loyal to Ish-bosheth and Joab hearing about this, went north to stop him. Radak contends that Joab and his army traveled north to extend David's territory. Ehrlich supposes that the Judeans and Israelites were heading to the sanctuary at Gibeon, for I Kings 3:4 states that there was "the great high place" there where Solomon offered a thousand burnt offerings on its altar.

49. An example is the battle between David and Goliath.

50. Granted that Abner was looking for a way to avoid killing Asahel and still saving Asahel's honor, but how could he suggests that Asahel kill another soldier? Abarbanel interprets Abner as saying do not kill him but take a trophy of his weapon.

brother to emphasize how despicable is Joab's act of revenge when he kills Abner in a later chapter.

Asahel's two brothers led forces against the fleeing army of Abner, but Abner persuaded Joab, one of his brothers, to call off the pursuit, and Joab agreed. In total, the army under Joab lost only nineteen men,[51] while three hundred and sixty of Abner's men died.[52]

Smith writes that since "the battle took place on Benjamite territory, where if anywhere Ish-bosheth's claim was valid [since his father Saul was a Benjamite], it seems more probable that David's men were acting on the offensive. David was seeking to extend his kingdom to the north of Judah. His piety towards Saul would not necessarily cause him to spare his successor."[53] If Smith is correct, this was the second attempt by David to move into Israelite territory, after his failure with Jabesh-gilead, both were thwarted.

WHAT DID THE PHILISTINES DO AFTER VANQUISHING SAUL'S ARMY?

The Bible gives no information about the Philistine actions or intentions after the war with Saul's army, when Saul was killed. It is likely that they were unconcerned about David's rule because they felt he was still a vassal of the Philistines, nor about that of Ish-bosheth because they saw he was weak (Hertzberg, Olam Hatanakh, and others). Segal and Smith propose that David may have asked Achish's permission to go to Hebron and become Judah's king. It is even possible that the Philistines demanded and received huge taxes from the two kingdoms. Smith adds that "their vassals should weaken each other by war was, of course, according to the wish of the Philistines."[54]

---

51. Rashi notes that it is impossible to decipher the Hebrew: was it nineteen men and Asahel or was Asahel included in the nineteen.

52. It is likely that David's troops were more successful because of the many battles they engaged in in prior years (Smith, *A Critical and Exegetical Commentary on the Book of Samuel*), 270. Gersonides contends that the numbers include the twelve men from each side who died in the duel, but the verse is unclear on this point.

53. Smith, *A Critical and Exegetical Commentary on the Book of Samuel*, 270

54. Ibid., 268.

More Attempts by David to Expand His Kingdom

II SAMUEL 3

Chapter 3 focuses on six events. (1) Verse 1, which many scholars feel belongs to chapter 2, simply states that the war between north and south continued for a long period. (2) David's family, his wives and children. (3) Abner's quarrel with Ish-bosheth. (4) Abner's negotiations with David. (5) The murder of Abner. (6) David's mourning Abner's death.

THE LENGTHY WAR

Verse 1 states that during the many battles between south and north, David's army grew stronger and stronger, while those of Abner became weaker. David used the seven years during which he was king of Judah to expand his alliances and land. He attempted an alliance with Jabesh-gilead, married the daughter of the king of Geshur whose son was Absalom,[55] and moved troops toward Gibeon. According to B. Mazar, it was during this period that he conquered Jerusalem (Olam Hatanakh).

DAVID'S FAMILY

David entered Hebron with two wives, but shortly thereafter took four more. Each of the six bore him a single son. No daughter is mentioned, although future chapters indicate he had a daughter. The marriage with the daughter of a non-Israelite Aramean king may have been prompted by politics, David wanting an alliance with a kingdom near Ish-bosheth's capital. As with some other kings

---

55. Later Absalom rebelled against his father David in an attempt to become king. It is possible that he felt he was fit for this position since he was both the son and grandson of kings (Olam Hatanakh).

of Judea and Israel, there is no hint that the non-Judean/Israelite women ever converted. Some even had their husbands build them a pagan temple so they could continue worshipping their gods. This is further proof that the idea of conversion did not exist during this early period of Israel's history, and the first mention of it is around 125 BCE.[56]

ABNER'S QUARREL WITH ISH-BOSHETH

Probably because he recognized that he was the power behind Ish-bosheth,[57] Abner felt he could ignore the practice that a king's harem passes to his successor and he took Rizpah, a concubine[58] of Saul, who by ancient right belonged to Ish-bosheth.[59] Ish-bosheth reprimanded Abner for his act and Abner was infuriated.[60] Abner insulted Ish-bosheth and asked how he could abuse him when he was protecting him against David. In his fury, Abner stated "as the Lord swore to David, so I will do for him."[61] Ish-bosheth was dumbfounded and did not reply because he feared Abner.

Did Abner believe that God promised the kingdom of Israel to David? *Midrash*

---

56. See Israel Drazin, *Unusual Bible Interpretations: Ruth, Esther, and Judith* (Jerusalem: Gefen Publishing House, 2016), 17–21.

57. Ehrlich notes that the narrator seems to have emphasized the weakness of Ish-bosheth by not including his name in his description of the encounter, as if he is so weak it is as if he does not exist.

58. Rashi explains that the difference between a concubine and a wife is that a wife is given a ketubah, a marriage contract that stipulates how much money a wife would receive in the event of a divorce or the husband's death. This may be an anachronism, for it is generally accepted by scholars that it was later rabbis who invented the idea of the ketubah to protect wives who they saw being discarded by husbands and left with nothing. Tradition states that the ketubah originated by Shimon ben Shetach around the first century BCE. See *Mishnah Sanhedrin* 2:1 and Maimonides, *Mishneh Torah, Laws of Women*, 1:4.

59. While the text states "go into," which could mean sex, Ehrlich takes it as marriage in this passage. A tragic story about Rizpah is found in 21:8–14. The right of successors to the wives and concubines of kings is found in 12:8, 16:21, and 1 Kings 2:22. It is likely that when Ish-bosheth saw Abner take Saul's concubine, he supposed that Abner was setting himself up to succeed him as king over Israel.

60. Abner was not unique. David's son Absalom did the same in 16:21, 22, as did Jacob's son Reuben in Genesis 35:22 and 49:3, 4. Ish-bosheth was not alone in suspecting someone of planning to rebel and become king. Solomon suspected his brother Adonijah when he wanted to take David's concubine as his wife, and he killed his brother (1 Kings 2:13–25).

61. Is Abner saying that he will now do all he can to help David be king of Israel? Did Ish-bosheth understand that this is what he was saying? The passage is unclear. Ehrlich comments: Scripture

Genesis Rabba supposes that he did.[62] Also Rashi, who imagined that when God promised Jacob in Genesis 35:11 that "kings (plural) will come out of your loins," God was referring to Ish-bosheth and David, and this is what Abner understood.

ABNER NEGOTIATES WITH DAVID

Abner's immediate response was to send David a message saying that if David would make a covenant with him, he would hand over the rule of Israel to him. It is possible, although unstated in scripture, that the two agreed that Abner would assume a leading role in David's army and that David would treat Ish-bosheth kindly (Kiel). David replied saying that the two would not meet unless Abner sent him his first wife Michal, King Saul's daughter, whom King Saul gave to Paltiel.[63]

Scripture does not state why David wanted Michal. It could be that he loved her, a desire to efface the insult which Saul had inflicted upon him by marrying her to another, a way to strengthen his claim as Saul's successor since he would be related to Saul as an in-law by marrying Michal, or any combination of these thoughts (Goldman).

Following protocol, he made his demand upon Ish-bosheth, knowing that Abner would force the king to comply.[64] "Give me my wife Michal whom I betrothed to me for a hundred Philistine foreskins."[65] Ish-bosheth complied, had her taken from her husband Paltiel, and had her brought to David. Scripture does not describe Michal's reaction, but tells us that her husband followed her, crying as he went, until Abner forced him to go home.[66]

The Bible does not reveal what happened to the marriage of Paltiel and Michal.

---

nowhere states that God "swore." Since ancient time people avenge their hurt by exaggerated notions about what bothers the person who hurt them.

62. *Midrash Genesis Rabba* 82 commenting on Genesis 35:11.

63. Since Michal was married to Paltiel, Torah law forbids David to marry her. The Torah states that a man who was married to a woman and divorced her and she married another, may not marry her again. See my discussion on this issue in my *Who Really Was the Biblical David?*, chapter 25.

64. David also did not want to reveal his negotiations with Abner to Ish-bosheth (Segal).

65. This is the number that Saul requested, although David gave him twice this number (1 Samuel 18:25).

66. Ehrlich contends that this was another of David's many deceitful schemes; that he was like the patriarch Jacob who tricked his brother Esau and took his father's blessing that Isaac intended for Esau.

Kiel suggests that as king, Ish-bosheth annulled that marriage, even as his father Saul annulled the marriage of Michal and David.

Abner laid the groundwork. He had spoken to the elders of Israel and Saul's tribe Benjamin before Michal was taken. He said that the elders had wanted David as their king, and now was an opportunity to fulfil their wishes.[67] He added that God had promised that David would save Israel from the Philistines.[68] He secured their acquiescence.

He brought Michal to David with an escort of twenty men and David arranged a feast for them. Abner left promising to speak to "all Israel" and have them make a covenant with David.[69] Scripture cites that Abner left in peace three times,[70] perhaps ironically, since he would soon be killed by Joab.

THE MURDER OF ABNER

Joab, David's commander, was not present during these negotiations, apparently knew nothing about them, and was still seething over Abner's killing of his brother Asahel. Joab returned from a great foray with much spoil, and it was then that he was told what transpired.[71] Joab complained to David and said he was sure that Abner was deceiving him and he came merely to discover the weaknesses of David's camp. Scripture does not record David's reply.[72] Without telling David, Joab sent a message to Abner requesting that he return.[73] When he returned, apparently thinking that David summoned him, Joab killed him "because of the blood of Asahel his brother."[74]

---

67. As usual, the Bible speak hyperbolically: perhaps only some elders wanted David to reign over Israel, but failed because Abner supported Ish-bosheth.

68. This alleged promise is not in the Bible, and may be a typical political ploy.

69. "all Israel" is another hyperbole and means "the elders of Israel."

70. Scripture uses the number three and seven frequently to highlight a subject.

71. It is plausible to suggest that David purposely arranged that Joab should be absent when Abner visited (Goldman).

72. This is a superb scriptural narrative style, for it leaves it to the reader to imagine various possibilities.

73. He most likely made believe the message was from David (Segal and Josephus, *Antiquities*, 7).

74. Archibald Robert Sterling Kennedy *Samuel* (T.C. & E.C. Clarke, 1905). While blood revenge is the sole reason Scripture gives for Joab's act, it is also likely that jealousy prompted his act as well as a passionate devotion to David.

DAVID MOURNS ABNER

By his act, Joab placed David in an untenable situation. Since Joab was his commander, it was likely that people would think that Joab murdered Abner with David's direction and approval. This could destroy his hope of uniting Judah and Israel under his rule. So David made a strong statement, apparently a public announcement, that he and his kingdom were in no way complicit in Abner's murder. He added a curse upon Joab "and upon all of his father's house"[75] that they are either unable to have children, be lepers, be disabled, die by a sword, or go hungry.[76]

David ordered Joab and his troops to tear their clothes, wear sackcloth,[77] and wail before Abner's body. He followed Abner's bier as a sign of respect. He buried Abner in Hebron, wept at his grave and gave a eulogy in which he emphasized that Abner was guiltless, and he was killed by iniquitous people. The people wept during the procession to the burial and after David's eulogy. David also publically refused to eat as a sign of mourning.

The people were impressed: "All the people [in Judah] and all [in the kingdom of] Israel understood that day that it was not because of the king that Abner the son of Ner was killed."[78]

And David did more. He called Abner a prince and berated the two sons of Zeruiah, but, significantly, he did not punish them.

David does not mention that Joab killed Abner as blood vengeance for the murder of Joab's brother. He may have refrained because blood vengeance does not apply when a soldier is killed in war.

Was David being hypocritical in his lament over Abner's death? Was this self-servingly mourning so that people would not blame him for the murder? We do not know. As it usually does, Scripture does not reveal people's thoughts, only their acts. We also do not know why David cursed all of Joab's family, apparently for generations, despite there certainly being many members of his family who

---

75. Verse 29.
76. Although unstated earlier, verse 30 mentions that Joab's brother Abishai joined him as a blood avenger in killing Abner.
77. A custom mentioned in Genesis 37:34.
78. Verse 37.

were innocent of Abner's murder. This may be typical biblical hyperbole and only mean: cursed be all who participated in the murder.

Why did David not punish Joab? Wouldn't this have added to his claim of innocence? S.L. Gordon, quoted by Goldman,[79] suggests that it may be that David relied on Joab who was his right-hand-man, and he was concerned that the army would stand by Joab its commander rather than him, or he was concerned that the people might have said he was eliminating himself of the one man who knew his guilt. It is also possible that Joab was not bothered by David's behavior and curses. He knew that David was not as distraught as he made out and that he had to act as he did to assure that he could be king over the united kingdom, and both understood that Joab would remain faithful to David.

Verse 22 states that Joab returned from a foray with much spoil, which he may have shared with the populace, who appreciated the gift, and who would be angered if David hurt their benefactor (Ehrlich). But David never forgot the difficulty into which Joab placed him. On his dying bed, when Joab was old and no longer powerful, David told his son and successor Solomon to kill him.[80]

---

79. S.L. Gordon, *Commentary on the Bible.*
80. 1 Kings 2:5 and 6.

The Treacherous Murder
of Ish-bosheth

II SAMUEL 4

Ish-bosheth, as we have seen, was powerless even when his general Abner supported him. Now that Abner had been murdered, he was as weak as a newborn lamb. He lost heart, "his hands became feeble, and all the Israelites were afraid."[81] It is possible that Ish-bosheth became frightened because Abner died in Hebron. He may have realized that for Abner to die in Hebron, he must have gone there to form a treaty with David; and if Abner went to form a treaty, all was lost. With this realization, Ish-bosheth sank into depression. He ceased acting as a king, he was lax with regard to his guards, which made it easy for conspirators to kill him (Ehrlich). He may have feared that his people, the Israelites, may have been frightened that David might seek vengeance against Ish-bosheth's supporters for refusing to accept David as their king (Altschuler).

THE MURDER OF ISH-BOSHETH

There were two captains of two troops, two brothers. They were members of Saul and Ish-bosheth's tribe Benjamin, and the family of both men fled.[82] These two

---

81. Verse 1.

82. It is unclear whether the brothers were captains of Ish Bosheth's forces at the time of this incident or were captains in the past. Ehrlich imagines that their family was disloyal to Saul and left the area even before the death of Saul. Segal is similar. He felt that when verse 2 states that they were commanders to Saul's son Ish-bosheth this is an error; they were commanders under his father Saul, but were disloyal to him, and they fled out of concern that Saul would kill them. Alternatively, Radak understands that only the two brothers fled, not their family, because, although unstated in the text, like Abner, they had a clash with Ish-bosheth.

men crept into Ish-bosheth's house,[83] while he lay on his bed, slew and beheaded him, and brought the head to David, acting like the Amalekite on II Samuel 1. They said: here is the head of Ish-bosheth who had sought to kill you.[84]

David reminded them that he had killed the Amalekite who also thought he was bringing David good tidings. "How much more, when wicked men killed a righteous man[85] in his own house on his bed."[86]

David ordered his soldiers to kill the brothers. They cut off the brothers' hands and feet, and hung them beside the pool in Hebron, apparently a public place for all to see and learn that regicide will be punished.[87] They took Ish-bosheth's head and buried it in the grave of Abner in Hebron.[88]

JONATHAN'S SON

The chapter also tells us parenthetically that Saul's son Jonathan had a son Mephibosheth, who was lame. When he was five years old and his nurse heard of Saul and Jonathan's death she rushed to flee, and in her haste, the boy fell and became lame. Thus, Saul's descendants were now all dead, except for a young lame boy, and the way was open for David to be king of the united tribes.

So ends the seven-year interregnum when David was king of Judah in Hebron, a period of civil war, upon which Scripture only sketches details, a time of unwarranted murders.[89]

---

83. Verse 6 lacks a word between "house" and "wheat": "they entered the house wheat merchants." Rashi and others understand the passage to be saying, they entered the house with wheat merchants, posing as two members of the group.
84. Scripture states nowhere that Ish-bosheth sought to kill David. There are at least two possible interpretations. Scripture very frequently does not state all the facts when incidences are mentioned, but reveals them later. Alternatively, this was a lie.
85. The Hebrew *ish tzaddik* can also be translated an innocent man.
86. Verse 11.
87. The Torah disallows the mistreatment of corpses. This is another instance of the Israelites not observing the Torah. See the Excursus following chapter 1 on *horaat shaah*.
88. His father's cousin.
89. Was it really seven years? Scripture frequently uses the numbers three, seven, and even forty, symbolically.

PART 2
David Is King of Judah and Israel

The next four chapters, 5–8, describe David's initial acts when he gained the crown over the united kingdom, the first time that the tribes were ruled by one man since the days of Moses, a situation that would end during the reign of his grandson Rehoboam.[1] He defeated the Philistines who had harassed the Israelites for decades, conquered Jerusalem which the tribes of Benjamin and Judah were unable to do in the past, made this central city his capital, brought the ark to Jerusalem so that the city would not only be the nation's political capital but also its spiritual center, extended the boundary of Israel, created diplomatic relations with other nations including taking a daughter of a neighboring king as his wife, and defeated other nations, feats that prompted a divine promise that his progeny would rule Israel forever.[2]

---

1. A close reading of Joshua shows that he was unable to keep the tribes together as a unit. See Israel Drazin, *Unusual Bible Interpretations: Joshua* (Jerusalem: Gefen Publishing House, 2014). 2. Those who read the Bible literally and who do not know or who need to believe that Scripture does not use hyperbole, take this prophecy as an assurance that a descendant of David will be the saving messiah. Actually, all that the prophecy is promising is that David's reign will last for a long time.

See 2 Samuel 7:16
Isa 9:7
Luke 1:31-32

David's Opening Gambits

II SAMUEL 5

Seven events occurred in chapter 5. (1) David was anointed ruler over the united kingdom of Judah and Israel, henceforeword called Israel.[3] (2) Two verses inform readers that David first became king at age 30 and remained king for forty years, in Hebron for seven years and three months and in Jerusalem for thirty-three years.[4] (3) The conquest of Jerusalem. (4) The turning of Jerusalem into the nation's capital and the building of David's house there. (5) David took more wives and concubines[5] and had sons and

---

3. This is the third time that David is anointed: first by Samuel, second by Judea, and lastly by the united tribes. Why was the united kingdom called Israel? It is clear that it could not be named Judah because this would insult the northern nation. David may have selected Israel, which was the name used by the northerners, as a shrewd diplomatic gesture, to make them feel he is considerate of them, or because all twelve tribes were descended from Jacob who was also called Israel.

4. The uses of the oft-repeated numbers, rather than precise figures: forty, three, and seven (as well as six months being twice three) – and if the numbers forty and seven years and six months are correct, the reign in Jerusalem should be thirty-two years and six months – seems to suggest that the author wanted to stress these numbers, but the use of these numbers raises the question whether they are correct. The suspicion that they are not correct is heightened when we realize that many people, including Moses and some kings, are said to have led the people for forty years, the number three reappears often in the chapter, and the number seven in the age David died, 70.

Since the numbers seven years and three months plus thirty-three years add up to forty years and six months, not forty years, the Greek translation Septuagint resolves this problem by writing that he was king in Jerusalem for thirty-two years and six months. However, we can see that the author wanted to use the traditional numbers and understand forty as a round number. The Babylonian Talmud, *Sanhedrin* 20a discusses the problem of Ish-bosheth being king in Israel for just two years while David ruled in Hebron for seven.

5. The rabbis in the Babylonian Talmud, *Sanhedrin* 21a define a "concubine" as a wife who is not given a ketubah, a document promising wives a financial settlement in the event of divorce or the husband's death. This cannot be correct since the giving of a ketubah was an institution

daughters.[6] (6) David battled the Philistines twice. (7) And if we include 6:1 among these events, David's troops increased to 30,000, ten times the number of Saul's army.[7]

THE ORDER OF THE EVENTS

While a cursory reading of the seven events seems to imply that they occurred soon after David was anointed king of the united tribes, a closer reading shows that some may have occurred during the seven years that he ruled in Hebron and some many years later. The first two address David being anointed as king and his age at the time and how long he ruled, but the latter statement focusing on the length of his rule speaks about the future. Some scholars think that David's conquest of Jerusalem and his defeat of the Philistines, items 3 and 6, occurred while David was in Hebron and was attempting to expand his territory and impress the northern nation of his energy, power, and successes. His making Jerusalem his capital, building his house there, taking wives and having children, items 4 and 5, did not occur immediately. For example, Solomon's birth is mentioned and he was born years later. Additionally, 1 Chronicles 3:1–9 states that six sons were born to David in Hebron and thirteen in Jerusalem. The total being nineteen "besides the sons of the concubines, and Tamar their sister.[8]

Goldman, Smith, and others suggest that the items are not in chronological order, and the conquest of Jerusalem occurred after David defeated the Philistines. This is reasonable because David would not want the Philistines to join and defend the Jebusites to stop David's expansion and rise to power. Smith adds that after

---

by the rabbis many generations later, and did not exist during the days of David. Tradition states it was formalized by Shimon ben Shetach around the first century BCE.

6. But only sons are mentioned. The Masoretic text states "from" Jerusalem, with the Hebrew letter *mem*, implying that the women were Jebusites, but this is an obvious error. The scribe mistook a *bet* for a *mem*, and the proper reading should be a *bet*, "in" Jerusalem. The version in 1 Chronicles 3:5 has the correct reading "in."

7. Many commentators agree that 6:1 belongs among the accomplishments of David in chapter 5. Chapter 6:2 begins a totally new subject, David wanting to bring the ark to his new capital. He was most likely unable to bring it to Hebron while he was king there because the ark was in the northern kingdom of Israel.

The number 30,000 contains three again.

That Saul's army comprised 3,000 men is mentioned in 1 Samuel 13:2 and 26:2.

8. Samuel 5 has the plural "sisters," rather than Chronicles' one, and only eleven sons.

the campaign with the Philistines, David felt "the necessity of possessing Jerusalem. While in the hands of the Canaanites, this city really cut his kingdom in two." Also, the chapter states that the Phoenician king of Tyre sent David material and workers to aid him in building his city and this most likely occurred after David had secured his kingdom for some time and impressed the king of Tyre.[9] Finally, item 7, about the number of his troops, most likely increased over the years, not immediately.

THE ANOINTING OF DAVID

With typical hyperbole, 5:1 states that "all the tribes came to Hebron to David, which is refined in verse 3 to "all the elders of Israel." Because 2:10 seems to say that Saul's son Ish-bosheth ruled two years, and since David is said to have been king in Hebron for seven and a half years, Kimchi proposes that they came five years after Ish-bosheth's death, with no ruler in Israel for the five years, but this is a minority opinion.[10]

The narrator has David say that the Israelites are related to them by blood, "we are your bone and your flesh." He may mean that they were all descendants of the patriarch Jacob, or that David led Saul's forces to victories during Saul's reign, diplomatically forgetting the dispute between Saul and David. The elders of the people said, "the Lord said concerning you that you will shepherd my people Israel and be a prince over Israel," perhaps suggesting that they knew that Samuel had anointed him many years previously or, more likely, since they showed no knowledge of this previously, they meant, "we now see that God wants you to be king."[11] However, Ehrlich interprets the elders' words to mean "from now on" we will be kin to one another.

The elders mentioned the word "you" three times in verse 2 to emphasize their desire that he rule over them (Kiel). David made a covenant with them, but

---

9. Olam Hatanakh states that the Phoenician king's help occurred near the end of David's life.
10. See the discussion about the two years in the commentary to 2:10.
11. Kiel notes that the elders' words "we are your bone and your flesh" could be interpreted that they accepted him as king even though he was a descendant of the Moabite Ruth. However, there is no recognition of Ruth as a person or as an ancestor of David in the books Samuel and Kings, as if the authors knew nothing about what the biblical book of Ruth states. The words are similar to those of Laban to Jacob in Genesis 29:14 and to the words in Genesis 2:23, Judges 9:2, and later in 19:13–14.

what the covenant was is unclear. Most likely it meant that David and the elders came to certain agreements concerning how David would rule and perhaps even limitations placed upon his rule. The acts were performed with some formality, for the verse states it was done before God.

THE CONQUEST OF JERUSALEM

The biblical Hebrew name of Jerusalem is without the Hebrew letter *yud* in it, even though the city's name is written today with a *yud* and is pronounced Yerushalayim. The spelling and pronunciation without the *yud* is also in ancient documents about the city, as in the El Amarna tablets of the fourteenth century BCE. Only Jeremiah 26:18 spells and pronounces the name with a *yud*.

Why is Jerusalem, along with Jeremiah, Joshua, and many other Hebrew names transliterated with a J when the Hebrew has a *yud*? It should be transliterated as an I or Y. This was the practice adopted several decades ago and has no significance. This manner of transliteration was not consistent, as we see that the Hebrew Yisrael was transliterated Israel and not Jisrael.

We have no knowledge of what the city's name means. Lots of suggestions have been made, but they are all speculation.[12]

Jerusalem was a good place for the nation's capital because it is located on the border between Judah and Israel and favored neither nation, and was on a high hill surrounded by steep valleys on three sides, which could be easily fortified. The Israelites were unable to take the city from the Jebusites until David did so. The tribes of Judah and Benjamin attempted to capture the city in Judges 1:8, 21, but failed.

When David began his assault, the Jebusites insulted him by saying, you can only beat us if you take away the blind and the lame. The boast is unclear. It may refer to two idols or to the Jebusites saying, we are so impregnable that we could even place lame and blind people upon our ramparts and you will be unable to conquer us. Josephus writes that the Jebusites placed the lame and blind upon their ramparts to taunt David.[13] Olam Hatanakh quotes Yadin who sees the wording

---

12. For example, *Genesis Rabbah*, 56 suggests that it is an abbreviation of *yireh shalom*, "see peace." Tradition states that Genesis 22:14's Mount Moriah was or was in Jerusalem. Zion was the southeastern part of Jerusalem (Segal). We no longer know what the word means.

13. Flavius Josephus, *The Antiquities of the Jews*, trans. William Whiston (Nashville, T.N.: Thomas

as the beginning of a magical curse, that the Bible omits, that prompted a god to inflict the Israelites with lameness and blindness if they pursued the assault. I Chronicles 11:5 goes further in omitting the taunt or curse entirely, perhaps, as is typical of Chronicles, its author(s) did not want to record anything that could show David in an unfavorable light.[14] The Aramaic Targum avoids this problem by creating a problematic theology when it translates "removing the sinners and the guilty," suggesting that the nation as a whole could not be successful unless they removed sinners and guilty people from their midst.

While the text states that David and his men conquered Jerusalem, suggesting that he used the same troops that accompanied him in prior times, Chronicles adds "and all Israel" to express that the united nation was involved in the capture of the future capital. Segal, Kiel, and others note that the conversation between the Jebusites and David suggests that before his assault, David attempted to negotiate a Jebusite surrender, but they rebuffed and insulted him.

THE TWO WARS WITH THE PHILISTINES

The Philistines warred with the Israelites since the Israelites entered Canaan and were generally successful. It is likely that they controlled the land and even forced the Israelites to pay tribute. This situation lasted until David totally defeated them.

It was the Philistines who initiated the war either because they saw that David was now king over all of the tribes or, if they attacked before David was anointed as ruler over Israel, because they saw he was attempting to extend his rule. David consulted God who told him to go fight for, "I will deliver them into your hands."[15] When the Philistines attacked again, David enquired again. This time he was told not to go up but to make a circuit behind them, and attack when he hears

---

Nelson, 2003. First published 1737), Book 7, 3, 1, 61.

14. Or, if it is a curse, there was a belief that words have effects, and if you say something bad, even if you do not want it to happen, it may happen. Even today, superstitious people spit three times (three again) to magically erase what has been said (three times is magical, as the Shulchan Arukh states, one should wash one's hands three times in the morning to remove the demons that ascended upon the hands during sleep).

15. While the Five Books of Moses tells the Israelites to use the Urim and Thummim, it is not used after the days of Moses, as if the Israelites knew nothing about this book. This chapter does not reveal how David consulted God.

The chapter does not say that David consulted God before attacking Jerusalem.

the mulberry trees rustling. David did as God instructed and totally defeated the Philistines. The Targum understands that the rustling would be "the angel of the Lord has gone forth to aid before you by killing the camp of the Philistines." Gersonides more realistically explains that David, either by divine advice or using a military tactic, waited until the wind rustled the trees so that the Philistines would not hear his advance.

Verse 21 presents a difficulty. It states that after the first battle, the Philistines ran and "left their images there [in the battle field], and David and his men took them." The word *atzabeihem*, "images,", is used to describe idols,[16] and 1 Chronicles 14:12 and the Targum here say explicitly, "they left their gods."[17] The problem is "and David and his men took them," which could imply that they took them to worship them. Chronicles changes *vayisa'iem*, "took them," to "burn them," to show that David and his soldiers observed Deuteronomy 7:5 which requires Israelites to burn idols. Ehrlich supposes that David and most Israelites of his era and later worshipped God as well as idols and he and his forces took the idols to worship them. He uses his understanding to explain why David needed to ask God again whether he should fight the Philistines, God had already told him to fight, he needed to ask since he had turned from God to worship idols and needed to find out if God would still help him.[18]

---

16. The word means "a man-made item" and is used by the Bible to disparage the idols.

17. Just as the Israelites took the ark into battle believing it would encourage God to help them (see 1 Samuel 4:4), the Philistines took their idols to war.

18. Ehrlich reads Isaiah 28:21 – "For the Lord will rise up as in Mount Perazim, he will be angry as in the valley of Gibeon" – the first battle between David and the Philistines was in Perazim – that the prophet is saying that God was angry with David after his first battle with the Philistines because of the idol worship, but God overcame the anger.

David Tries Twice to Bring the Ark to Jerusalem

II SAMUEL 6

After being accepted as king over the now united tribes, defeating the Philistines in two battles and destroying their ability to wage war against Israel in the future, capturing Jerusalem and making the city his capital, David decided to bring the ark to Jerusalem, apparently, although unstated in Scripture, to aggrandize his image to show the northern tribes that he could do what Saul was unable to do, and make the city his political and spiritual capital. As usual, this chapter raises a number of questions: (1) What is the significance of the ark? (2) Why didn't Saul bring the ark to his capital? (3) Uzzah, one of the men who was accompanying the ark to Jerusalem was killed by God; what did he do that was wrong? (4) Was it Uzzah who acted improperly, or David? (5) The chapter states that God was angry; how can the all-wise and all-powerful deity give in to an emotion? (6) Why does the narrator tell his readers about the fight between David and his wife Michal?

THE ARK OF GOD

I discussed the ark of God in chapter 4 of my book *Who Was the Biblical Prophet Samuel?* and will not repeat the full discussion here. Briefly stated, the word ark, in Hebrew *aron*, is mentioned 201 times in the Hebrew Bible, including once where Scripture stated Joseph's body was placed in an ark.[19] The ark in Moses's day was a wooden box covered in gold about four feet long by thirty inches. It was carried

---

19. Genesis 50:26. The Torah uses the word *tevah* for the ark in which Noah was saved from the flood in Genesis 6:14 and Moses saved from the Nile in Exodus 2:3.

with staves that remained in place even when the ark was not being moved. Two carved cherubim[20] sat atop the cover of the ark. The two tablets of the Decalogue (Ten Commandments) were placed in the ark in accordance with the ancient custom of other nations of setting documents and agreements between kingdoms at the feet of their god.[21] Some scholars suggest that the cherubim on top of the ark served as the seat upon which God sat and the ark served as the footstool of God. Exodus 25:22 relates that God told Moses he would meet with him at the ark and would speak with him between the cherubim. Jeremiah 3:16–17 states that in the future Jerusalem and not the ark will be the seat of the Lord.

Since God was understood to sit atop the ark, and God was powerful, the ancient Israelites felt that they should bring the ark to the battlefield so that God could be there to help them. Joshua did so at Jericho (Joshua 3:6, 6:6) and the Israelites did it I Samuel 4 and in II Samuel 11.

Curiously, the cherubim upon which scholars contended God sat mysteriously disappeared without comment or explanation, for when Solomon built his temple and placed the ark inside, he built new cherubim.[22]

In this chapter, although verse 2 states "the Lord of hosts that sits upon the cherubim," there is no other mention of the cherubim. It is as if the cherubim no longer existed and the quoted phrase refers to a past event, or it is a phrase added to the text by some scribe, but was not in the original text. This would explain why Solomon had to build new cherubim.

It is unclear whether the people believed that God was literally present on top of the ark and used it as a footstool, or the people considered the ark as only a symbol of the divine presence who was not limited to a particular area.

WHY DIDN'T SAUL BRING THE ARK TO HIS CAPITAL?

We do not know. The book of Samuel is remarkably unkind to Saul, even though many dispassionate readers reading what the narrator tells about Saul and his

---

20. These were two winged figures whose appearance is in dispute. They may have looked like children or may have represented angels. The word cherubim is mentioned ninety-one times in the Hebrew Bible.

21. Gershom Scholem, *Encyclopedia Judaica*, vol. 3 (Jerusalem: Keter, 1972). That the ark contained the Decalogue and perhaps even the Torah is not mentioned. Is this another indication that the Samuel author did not know about the Torah?

22. I Kings 6:23–28.

conflicts with Samuel and David, especially Samuel, feel that the book treats Israel's first king unfairly. We do not know his age when he became king, how long he reigned,[23] his age at his death, whether he had a castle or even a large house as his home, and his activities are only hinted at best. Thus it is not surprising that we know nothing about his relationship with the ark.

WHAT MISDEED DID UZZAH COMMIT?

Without telling readers why David did so, Scripture states that David arose and went with all the people that were with him to bring the ark of God from Kiriath-jearim to Jerusalem.[24] I Chronicles 13 describes David's preparations for the trip in great detail. II Samuel lacks this information and it does not state why the ark was not brought out of Kiriath-jearim sooner or why the ark was not used in any worship service while it was in Kiriath-jearim. It is likely that it was inaccessible because the city was controlled by the Philistines. Now that David had defeated the Philistines, he was able to reacquire the ark.[25]

David had the ark placed on a new cart and the cart was led toward Jerusalem with much music, accompanied by many celebrating people including Uzzah, the son or grandson of the man who had been assigned the responsibility to guard the ark when it was placed in Kiriath-jearim some twenty years earlier.

Then Uzzah was killed. The chapter does not say clearly why he was killed. The

---

23. Although the length of his reign may have been mentioned in the text in 13:1 before the verse lost words.

24. The story of the capture of the ark by the Philistines is told in I Samuel 4, how God punished the Philistines in I Samuel 5, the Philistine attempt to return the ark to Israel in a new cart with two milch kine and with gifts in chapter 6. Chapter 6 tells the poor reaction of the Israelites and God killing fifty thousand Israelites because of their behavior, and how the ark was then transferred to Kiriath-jearim where it remained, apparently unused, for twenty years. Why did God kill fifty thousand men? The number, as usual, is most likely an exaggeration. It is possible, even likely, that as stated in I Samuel 5, a devastating plague struck the Philistine cities while the ark happened to be there and the germs infected the ark. The Philistines and Israelites thought the plague was a divine punishment, although it was a natural occurrence. When the infected ark reached the Israelite territory it was still carrying the germs, and it was these germs that killed the multitude of Israelites as it had done to the Philistines. The fact that the ark was considered a sacred item does not protect it from germs. Similarly, today, people should cease kissing the Torah in synagogues, even placing a book on the Torah and kissing the book or another item, for it is likely that those who kissed the Torah with their mouths placed germs on the Torah.

25. This is the view of A.R.S. Kennedy, *Samuel*.

book only states "When they came to the threshing-floor of Nacon, Uzzah put forth … to God's ark, and took hold of it, for the oxen stumbled." Where I put dots, a word or words seem to be missing. The implication is that Uzzah put forth his hand. Verse 7 states "God smote him there *al hashal*." Commentators define the two words as "for his error," but the text does not say who committed the error, David or Uzzah. It also does not state why an error should be punished by death.

Many explanations have been offered to explain Uzzah's demise, including: (1) Uzzah was culpable because he showed disrespect to the ark when he touched it in violation of Numbers 4:15, even though his intention was good, for he may have thought that since the oxen stumbled, the ark would topple over. (2) Uzzah should have had trust that God would not allow the ark to fall (the view of Rashi). (3) Uzzah showed undue respect for the ark as the Israelites did in 1 Samuel 6:19, where thousands died. (4) David, not Uzzah, was the guilty party for ordering the ark to be transported by a cart. Numbers 3:31 mandates that the ark may only be borne by Levites who should carry it on their shoulders. Should we conclude that David did not know this law even though he knew about the Torah? Or is this still another indication, as with the over three dozen indications we noted in the book of Samuel, that the author of Samuel knew nothing about the Torah of Moses?

David "was afraid of the Lord that day,"[26] and left the ark with Obed-edom the Gittite.[27] Three months later, David was told that God blessed his house because of the ark, and David resumed his goal to bring the ark to Jerusalem. This time, he was very cautious: when they bore the ark six paces, sacrifices were offered to God.[28]

WHY DOES THIS BOOK STATE THAT GOD BECAME ANGRY AT WHAT TRANSPIRED?

Although it appears that David had good intentions when he attempted twice to

---

26. Verse 9.

27. While "Gittite" seems to indicate that Obed-edom was a Philistine from Gath, 1 Chronicles 15: 18, 24, and 26: 4ff, states he was a Levite from the family of Korah whom the book of Numbers assigns responsibility for carrying the ark.

28. The text states that they bore the ark, which could mean that they still carried it on a wagon contrary to Numbers, but 1 Chronicles 15:15 states that now Levites carried it on their shoulders as required by the Torah. One could ask, since according to Chronicles Uzzah died because the ark was carried by a wagon, why doesn't the chapter inform readers that David corrected his mistake? Isn't this an indication that the author of this chapter did not think that Uzzah's death was a result of a violation of Torah law?

transport the ark to his new capital, God became angry during his first attempt. Maimonides explains that the all-powerful and all-wise deity has no human emotions and that the Bible states that he does become angry to frighten the people not to misbehave. We should therefore understand that the author is telling us that David's first attempt to bring the ark to Jerusalem, although with good intentions, was not done correctly. We should also understand that Uzzah's death was a natural event, although we do not know what caused his death. Apparently, the Samuel author hid the truth to focus on his point that we need to behave properly.

DAVID BERATES HIS WIFE MICHAL

David had insisted in chapter 3 that the Israelites return his first wife Michal before he would consider accepting the kingship over all the tribes, apparently to show that he was related by marriage to Saul and had a claim on being Saul's successor. Now that he had secured his objective, he had no more strategic use of Michal. Thus, during the celebratory march of the bringing of the ark to Jerusalem, when she told him that his dancing almost naked before the throng of people was indecent,[29] he responded with fierce anger. He said that God chose him not her father.

The chapter concludes: "And Michal, Saul's daughter, had no child until the day of her death." Rashi comments that David was so angered that he ceased having sexual relations with Michal. Whether this is the true meaning of the verse, it is clear that the author of Samuel is making it clear that Saul's dynasty was over; he had no descendants.[30]

SUMMARY

While being very interested in bringing the ark to his newly established capital, David seems to have violated Numbers 3:31 which mandates that only Levites may carry the ark and only on their shoulders, and not in a wagon, a manner of

---

29. Michal's words are, "How did the king of Israel honor himself today by uncovering himself in the eyes of the handmaids of his servants." Does "handmaids of his servants" denote the lowest element of David's society, or is Michal, who loved David expressing jealousy? See Drazin, *Who Really Was the Biblical David?*.

30. A Midrash insists that Mordecai in the book of Esther was a descendant of Saul.

transport used previously by the Philistines and which David was copying, as if he or/and the author of Samuel had no idea about the Torah of Moses. Rather than correcting his behavior, it appears that he resorted to what one might call a bribe, sacrifices, to assure that another Israelite would not be killed by God. Additionally, II Samuel does not state that when David tried a second time, this time successfully, to bring the ark to Jerusalem, he had Levites carry the ark on their shoulders as Numbers dictates.

Like Samuel before him,[31] although not a priest, David garbed himself in the priestly ephod when he danced "before the Lord with all his might."[32]

While the chapter is devoted to the ark, no mention is made of the contents of the ark, the Decalogue, and, according to some opinions, the Torah. Is this another indication that Samuel's author did not know about the Torah, and the only significance David and the Israelites saw for the ark was its association in some way with God, that the ark was brought to bring God to protect Israel, and people do not protect themselves by obeying Torah law?

---

31. I Samuel 2:18.
32. Verse 14.

Three Reports on Why David Was Forbidden to Build a Temple

II SAMUEL 7

We have seen in my prior volumes on the biblical book of Samuel that Scripture frequently offers duplicate accounts of an event with one account being strikingly different than the other.[33] We can accept either one as true. As Abraham ibn Ezra wrote in his two introductions to his commentary to the Torah, Jewish tradition does not preclude people from seeking an interpretation that seems reasonable to them, as long as it does not contradict the behavior required by halakhah (Jewish law). One example is found in three different scriptural books that offer three diverse, seemingly irreconcilable explanations as to why God forbade David to build a temple in Jerusalem.

DAVID WANTS TO BUILD A TEMPLE

The first house of God, built by Moses, was a simple portable tent structure. It remained a tent or tent-like structure for hundreds of years, even after the Israelites settled in Canaan and built permanent houses for themselves. The only partial exception was the tabernacle at Shilo, before and during part of the life of the prophet Samuel, which was a semi-permanent building.

It was as if the biblical sanctuary tent was purposely constructed in a non-permanent fashion to emphasize that this was not a home in which a non-corporeal God could possibly dwell. It was a temporary "Meeting House," a name the Bible itself gave the tent. The wise among the Israelites understood that God did not live or even visit there; it was a place where people could *feel* in touch with God and

---

33. This happened frequently in Samuel, but it also occurred in the Five Books of Moses.

from which they could spiritually or emotionally – but not physically – connect with Him.

After years of warfare,[34] when David felt that he had brought peace to his country and that his people could dwell in fine luxurious houses in peace, he thought of building a large palace for himself, but he felt that it was improper that he and his people should dwell in exquisite houses while only a feeble, impermanent, primitive tent was set aside for the worship of God.

SAMUEL'S REPORT

In Samuel 7, God rejected David's offer. God sent the prophet Nathan to David and said that the building of a permanent structure would go against the long history of the non-permanent tent. "I have not dwelt in a house since the day I brought up the people of Israel from Egypt to this day, but I have been moving about in a tent for my dwelling." Although not stated explicitly, the prophet is apparently informing David what is indicated above. More than a breach of tradition, the use of a stable building might affect how the people perceived God. They could come to believe that God was actually dwelling in the house, even as humans live in their homes. Thus, the building of the prominent "house of God," while well meaning, would teach the people an improper idea about God.

THE DIVINE RESPONSE IN I KINGS 5:3

The book of Kings, on the other hand, avoids the theological problem in favor of a practical rationale. Solomon informed Hiram the king of Tyre, "You know that David my father could not build a house for the name of the Lord his God because of the warfare with his enemies who surrounded him, until the Lord put them under the soles of his feet." In other words, according to Kings, David was unable to build a house of God because he was preoccupied with wars.[35]

---

34. We do not know when David felt the need to build a temple, but it seems that it was before the birth of Solomon since verse 12, I Chronicles 22:9ff and I Kings 18:15ff seem to state that David will have a child in the future that will build the temple (Goldman).

35. Arguably, this statement should be understood as not contradicting what is stated in Samuel. Solomon gave this reason to Hiram rather than the theological reason because the theological reason might offend Hiram who believed in the presence of his god.

THE RATIONALE IN I CHRONICLES 22:8

Chronicles contains a third idea. It states that David was not fit to build the Temple because he was a man of blood and it is inappropriate to associate bloodshed with the Temple. In the book, David summons his son Solomon and tells him that he had wanted to construct a house for God, but "the word of the Lord" came to him and told him, "You have shed much blood and have waged great wars; you shall not build a house to my name because you have shed so much blood before me upon the earth."[36]

HOW CAN WE RECONCILE THE THREE REPORTS?

There are two ways to square the three accounts. These two approaches to resolving conflicting statements are the two approaches employed by the Talmuds frequently when two rabbis offer divergent statements. The first approach, in essence, states that the two have the same view but are addressing different facts. The second approach accepts the notion that talmudic rabbis can disagree. Generally speaking, Ashkenazic rabbis, such as Rashi and Tosaphot, prefer the former view and Sephardic teachers, such as Maimonides, the latter.

1. Consistent with the first methodology, that there is no difference, they may all be describing the same reason from different angles. The Bible may be telling us that basically God, as Maimonides teaches in his *Guide of the Perplexed* 3:32, does not need or even want a temple or temple sacrifices. People should instead seek God by trying to know God through understanding the sciences of the universe and by living a proper life with others. If a temple and sacrifices are necessary as a concession to the primitive notions of people, as Maimonides taught, worship in the temple should be as limited as possible. One way of limiting it is by cutting down on the types of sacrifices that may be offered and by restricting where and when they can be offered. Another way, as seemingly indicated in Samuel, is by keeping the temple small and in an impermanent state. However, since the people would not listen to reason, David, according to Kings, was stopped from building a temple because he was too occupied with warfare, and warfare is the opposite of what a temple should stand for.

---

36. 1 Chronicles 22:8.

Chronicles, which speaks of the shedding of blood, could be seen as saying the same thing as Kings, for war is wrong since it results in the shedding of blood.

2. Alternatively, following the second method of analysis, we can accept that the three accounts are three distinct irreconcilable views. The frequently used talmudic response to rabbinical controversies, *eilu va'eilu divrei Elohim chayim,* "both are words of the living God," can be applied here. In other words, the rabbis recognized that people do not always agree and there may be validity in more than one view even when the opinions are diametrically opposed and offer contradictory beliefs.

DID DAVID ACT IMPROPERLY?

This discussion could be seen to suggest that David did not always behave correctly. Other biblical incidents, especially his seduction of Bat-sheba and the murder of her husband and the members of his platoon, seem to confirm this conclusion. How can we reconcile this assessment with the view in the Babylonian Talmud, *Shabbat* 56a, which states that "Whoever says that David sinned errs, for it is said (1 Samuel 18:14) 'And David behaved himself wisely in all his ways: and the Lord was with him'"? Again, we seem to have conflicting assessments and we can resolve them by using the above-mentioned two methods.

First, we can argue that there is no conflict between those rabbis who insist that David committed no wrong and those who say the opposite. We can contend that although it may appear that David did wrong, circumstances that were not stated in the Bible exonerated his deeds. Or, we can acknowledge that he acted improperly, but say that he atoned for his misdeeds and the atonement cleansed him, as if he never did wrong. Both solutions assert that there is no disagreement between the apparently different rabbinical views; one addresses the situation as it appears to be – that David did wrong – while the other states what is not apparent, that he was actually doing what is proper; alternatively, one focuses on the situation prior to the repentance and the second after David repented.

The second solution recognizes that we are presented with conflicting ideas. It is possible, even likely, that the talmudic rabbis made the positive statement for the masses of Jews who could not think that such a heroic figure like David, the author of the sacred Psalms, could ever do wrong.

However, at the same time, the talmudic statement also suggests to the deeper thinker, who has read the Bible and knows that at times David did wrong, that one needs to evaluate the entire life of the king, the good and the bad, and realize that although he, like all humans, acted improperly at times, he was a great leader, and we should not dwell overmuch on his improper behavior. This solution helps us see that we too, although we act improperly at times, should not give up on ourselves, but continue to strive to improve and live a proper and fulfilling life.

David Chose His Staff

II SAMUEL 8

David continued to expand his kingdom. He engaged in wars, captured Philistine cities, killed many Moabite people,[37] established dominion as far as the river Euphrates, smote the Arameans and forced them and many other nations to pay tribute to him, made the Edomites servants, disabled hundreds of horses by cutting the sinews of hind legs apparently to stop them being used in chariots in war against Israel,[38] took 1,700 horsemen from a Syrian king,[39] "and the Lord gave David victories wherever he went."[40] David's principle officers are named, including Joab who was over his army, and Benaiah who commanded the Cherethites and Pelethites; "and David's sons were priests (cohanim)." With this information, the book of Samuel ends the report of David's public affairs. Henceforth, we will see private matters, many of which are tragic (Driver).

DID DAVID ACT VICIOUSLY?

Verse 2 states, "And David smote Moab. He measured them[41] with a line (Targum,

---

37. We are not told why David (or Saul in 1 Samuel 14:47) fought against Moab or why he treated the inhabitants so badly.

38. Rashi and Radak state he did this to four hundred horses. They and Altschuler state that David wanted to diminish the capacity of the foreign nation to wage war against Israel so he had to remove their battle horses, and although it is improper to generally harm animals, as stated in Deuteronomy 20:19, David could not take them to his own stables because Deuteronomy 17:16 forbids kings to have many horses. This explanation is unlikely since David ignored other prohibitions in the Torah and may not have even known of the existence of the Torah.

39. What did David do with these soldiers? The chapter does not say. Apparently, he incorporated them into his own army. See the discussion on the Cherethites and Pelethites.

40. Verse 6 and 14.

41. The verse is obscure: who are "them"? Are they the entire Moabite population, men, women, and children? Where they just all the men in the population or only the warriors?

by lots) lying them down on the ground. He measured two lines to kill, and one full line to keep alive." This verse seems to say that David killed two thirds of the Moabites after defeating them, making them lie down in rows and only allowing the third person in the row to live. This horrific event is inexplicable and inhuman, especially if we recall that the book of Ruth states that David was descended from Ruth the Moabite.[42] Also, the Israelites are told in Deuteronomy 2:9 "Do not engage in war with them for I will not give you his land as a possession." Additionally, in 1 Samuel 22:3f, David had friendly relations with the Moabites and left his family with the king for protection against Saul. Rashi attempts to explain the behavior by quoting a Midrash on 22:4 that states that after David left his family with the Moabite king, the king had them killed. But does this justify his reaction in this chapter, the mass murders of captives? Goldman supposes that he only killed the males, but this only mitigates the murders slightly. 1 Chronicles does not record this incident, most likely because its intent is to describe David in a favorable light.

WHO WERE THE CHERETHITES AND PELETHITES?

In several prior chapters and in future chapters, certain biblical figures were identified as being from non-Israelite nations, such as Uriah the Hittite, the first husband of David's later wife Bat-sheba. This bothered the rabbis. Surely, they wanted to think, these men were Israelites but their names were associated with another nation perhaps because they lived in that area, or had one of their houses in the area, or they performed a highly recognized, but now forgotten, act in that country. Or, if they were non-Israelites, surely they must have converted to Judaism, even though there is no indication in the Bible that they converted or that a system of conversion existed before the mid-second century BCE.[43] Some scholars and some rabbis recognize the plain meaning of the text; these were non-Israelites.

The same concerns exist regarding the Cherethites and Pelethites. Traditional sources insist these were not non-Israelites. The Babylonian Talmud *Berakhot* 4a

---

42. Since the books of Samuel and Kings do not mention David's descent from the Moabite Ruth and since David acted so cruelly with the Moabites here, it seems likely that the story of David being descended from Ruth is problematical and possibly untrue.

43. See my detailed essay on the subject of conversion, "Did Ruth Convert," in Israel Drazin, *Unusual Bible Interpretations: Ruth, Esther, and Judith* (Jerusalem: Gefen Publishing House, 2016), 17–21.

and *Sanhedrin* 15b state that Benaiah was in charge of the Urim and Thummim, not military men. The Aramaic Targum writes he was appointed over the archers and the slingers. Rashi and Radak quote both views, and Altschuler mentions the Targum.

In contrast, 1 Chronicles 18:17 retains Cherethites and Pelethites without any explanation. Goldman notes that they are mentioned together with the Gittites and were most likely non-Israelite mercenary soldiers. McCarter notes that 23:23 states that Benaiah was placed over David's bodyguard, so this must have been the function of the two groups.[44] Ehrlich notes reasonably that the two names are always joined together, they only served David and are not mentioned as serving other kings, and any decision as to their identity is pure guesswork.[45]

HOW COULD DAVID'S SONS BE PRIESTS?

Exodus 28:1 states that only Aaron and his descendants may serve as priests. McCarter suggests that this shows that in David's era, priests were not limited to the family of Aaron, Moses's brother. However, the traditional commentators translate *cohanim* as "officials." Some scholars note that during the Davidic era (before David, and likely long afterwards), before and after the building of a temple in Jerusalem, there were many *bamot*, "high places," throughout the land, where altars were placed and sacrifices offered, and *cohanim* who were not from the family of Moses' brother Aaron, functioned in these places (Kiel).

---

44. Benaiah became the head of Solomon's army after his brother Joab, 1 Kings 2:35, 4:4.
45. They are also mentioned in 15:18, 20:7 and 23, and 1 Kings 1:38 and 44.

PART 3
David Settles Into His Role as King of All Israel

David and Jonathan's Son

II SAMUEL 9

David asked if there were any descendants of Saul still living so that he could "show him kindness for Jonathan's sake." A servant of Saul's house was summoned, Ziba, who told David that Jonathan's son Mephibosheth was alive and that he was lame. We will see in a later chapter that Ziba was a bad man who was seeking to advance his personal interests and those of his family, and it is well to read this chapter with this understanding.[1] For example, why did Ziba mention that Mephibosheth was lame when David did not ask about his health? Did he do so to take advantage of the situation? Perhaps he was saying that Mephibosheth was incapable of managing the estate. Or perhaps the narrator mentioned this disability twice, by Ziba and as an aside at the chapter end, to hint why David did not kill him: both his disability and David keeping him close to watch him lessened the possibility that he would lead a rebellion.

DAVID, ZIBA, AND MEPHIBOSHETH

When Ziba told David where Mephibosheth was located, David fetched him. When he arrived, Mephibosheth was fearful, and David needed to assure him that he meant him no harm. He told Mephibosheth that he wanted him to "eat bread [meaning meals] at my table continually." He also told Mephibosheth that he was restoring Saul's land to him and was doing so "for Jonathan your father's sake."[2] Mephibosheth bowed down and said, "What is your servant that you should look upon such a dead dog as I am?"

---

1. In 16:3, Ziba tells David that Mephibosheth is conspiring against him with the goal to become king.
2. With Saul's death, apparently by the then existing rules, the dead king's wealth, including his wives, revert to the new king.

David called Ziba, told him about the huge gift of property to Mephibosheth, that Mephibosheth would be eating at the king's table, and instructed him to care for Mephibosheth's property. The chapter reveals that Ziba had fifteen sons and twenty servants, all Mephibosheth's servants, thereby letting readers know that Mephibosheth's land, land previously owned by King Saul, was huge, requiring at least thirty-five workers. This information reveals that Ziba and his family had been consuming the produce of the fields, and Mephibosheth did not complain to David out of fear for his life by the king (Ehrlich). The chapter also states that Mephibosheth had a son Mica. Mephibosheth, and presumably his son and perhaps his wife or wives, did not dwell on the estate but in Jerusalem, probably as a result of David's command. The chapter ends by reminding readers that Mephibosheth was lame on both feet.

WHEN DID DAVID EXPRESS CONCERN ABOUT JONATHAN'S SON?

Goldman felt that this incident must have occurred at least fourteen years after the death of Saul, for at that time Mephibosheth was five years old, as indicated in 4:4, and now he is old enough to have a young son, Mica, as recorded in verse 12. Why David waited so long to keep his promise to Jonathan to look after his children (1 Samuel 20:15) is not told. We were told that Jonathan loved David in 1 Samuel 20: 17, but not the reverse. This incident seems to suggest that David did not feel that close to Jonathan.[3] It reminds us that both Jonathan and Michal loved David, but it is likely that his feelings about them were strategic, not emotional.

WHY DID DAVID WANT MEPHIBOSHETH IN
JERUSALEM EATING AT HIS TABLE?

The ancient practice was for a newly enthroned king to kill all possible rivals. Abimelech, for example, killed his seventy brothers in Judges 9:5 and David's son Solomon killed his brother and others in 1 Kings 2; both did so in fear that the men might attempt to usurp them. Ehrlich supposes it likely that David had intended to eradicate all of Saul's family but did not kill Mephibosheth because

---

3. Noting that this chapter does not follow what is stated in chapter 8 and does not lead into chapter 10, Ehrlich supposes that it is misplaced and the event occurred seven years earlier after David became king of the united tribes, and perhaps as early as when he began to rule Judah. Goldman's dating that takes Mephibosheth's age into account seems more reasonable.

his lameness weakened his ability to gain supporters to usurp him; yet as an extra caution, he wanted to keep an eye on him.

WHAT WAS MEPHIBOSHETH'S REACTION?

Mephibosheth approached David with fear when initially summoned, and David had to assure him he wanted what was best for him because of his father Jonathan. It is likely that Mephibosheth was not convinced since it was now more than a decade since his father's death, and David had many opportunities to treat him well, but did not do so. As he left the interview, Mephibosheth was careful to act humbly, calling himself a servant and dog, not a prince.

David Continues His Wars

II SAMUEL 10

When Nahash the king of Ammon died and Hanun his son reigned in his stead, David recalled that Nahash had shown kindness to him, so he sent officials to Hanun in Ammon to offer him condolences. Hanun misunderstood the gesture and waged war against Israel, a war that led to the drama of David and Bat-sheba.

HANUN MISUNDERSTANDS DAVID'S MESSAGE

Scripture does not tell us what kindness Nahash did for David. We encountered Nahash previously in 1 Samuel 11 when he threatened the Israelite city of Jabesh-gilead. At that time King Saul came to the aid of this city and defeated Nahash. Ehrlich, Goldman, and others suppose that as an enemy of Saul, Nahash may have helped David in his conflicts with Saul and his successor Ish-bosheth.

Hanun, like Rehoboam the son of Solomon in 1 Kings 12, took counsel from unwise counselors with dire results.[4] While David meant well, Hanun's advisors, most likely saw how David had mistreated the Moabites and did not see him treat any nation neighboring Israel kindly, advised the king that David's messengers must have been sent to spy on Ammon to prepare for a future attack.[5] Hanun, perhaps feeling insulted, abused the messengers by cutting half their beards, likely on one side of their face, and cut their clothes so that their buttocks could be seen.

Hanun realized that David would not accept the insult calmly, that his act would result in war. He hired mercenaries, including 20,000 Arameans and 13,000 others. David sent his cousin Joab to fight them. Joab found himself surrounded.

---

4. This taking of bad advice with dire results is similar to Rehoboam, son of Solomon, taking advice from his young, probably inexperienced advisors, in 1 Kings 12.
5. This would be similar to Joshua's action before attacking Jericho in Joshua 2.

One enemy troop was in front of his army and another in back. Joab divided the troops. He led the forces against the Aramean mercenaries, maybe thinking them more formidable, and placed his brother Abishai against the troops of Ammon. They were somewhat successful. The Arameans fled back to their country and the Ammonites ran back to their city.

However, the Arameans regrouped and attacked. David himself led the battle against them and defeated them, and they became vassals to David. But Ammon was not vanquished.[6]

---

6. It seems likely that David knew he was a better military commander than his cousins and needing to defeat the Armenians led the forces himself.

PART 4
The Bat-sheba Affair

David's acts in these two chapters have consequences that destroy his future life and the lives of his family.

David Commits Adultery and Murder

II SAMUEL 11 – 12

Chapters 11 and 12 relate that David remained in the luxury of his palace while his general Joab led his forces against the nation of Ammon across the Jordan River. Sieges last usually months, sometimes years, and it is understandable that a king would not want to waste time outside a besieged enemy fortress. During the night, David spied a woman, saw she was beautiful, sent his guard to fetch her, bedded her, and sent her home.[1] The woman was Bat-sheba, the wife of Uriah. Uriah was a soldier, away with the fighting forces.[2]

BAT-SHEBA IS PREGNANT

Not long thereafter, Bat-sheba sent a message to the king telling him that she was pregnant. David summoned Uriah and ordered him to report about the siege. He

---

1. The Bible does not disclose the cruelty of David's behavior toward Bat-sheba other than to describe that he sent his guard for her. This was no seduction. Nor was any love expressed when he sent her back home with guards. However, the cruelty of his act is dramatically shown by the way the prophet Nathan describes it in his parable of the rich man who had many lambs, who stole the only young lamb of a poor man – a lamb that loved to sleep in the bosom of its owner and was never intended for slaughter – and then slaughtered the sheep (obviously against its will) and gave it to a guest to eat.

2. Both David and Bat-sheba were on the roofs of their houses. Why was Bat-sheba bathing naked in a place where people could see her? Was she hoping that David would see her and summon her? We do not know. However, when the text states that David saw a woman bathing from the roof, this could mean that he saw her bathing on the roof of her own house, or more likely, that he saw her bathing (in her apartment) by being able to see her while he was on his roof, through a window in her bathing area, and Bat-sheba did not know that a person could stand on his own roof and see her, because most houses were not as high as David's house.

hoped to entice Uriah to sleep with his wife and believe that the child that would be born is his own. Uriah arrived and reported, but, perhaps suspicious of the king, he did not return home. David tried four times to have him go to Bat-sheba, but he refused.

David sent Uriah back to the army with a secret message to Joab to arrange to have Uriah killed. Joab did as David commanded. "And when the mourning [of Bat-sheba for her husband] was past, David sent and took her to his house, and she became his wife, and bore him a son. But the thing that David did displeased the Lord."

David's punishment is outlined in 12:10 and 11. Nathan the prophet predicts, "the sword will never depart from your house. . . . I will take your wives before your eyes and give them to your neighbor, and he will lie with your wives in the sight of the sun."[3] Thus, while David caused the death of Uriah and his platoon, whom Joab ordered to attack the besieged wall where they would surely be killed, many of his children would be killed, and while he debauched one man's wife, many of his wives would be debauched. The Babylonian Talmud, *Yoma* 22b, adds that David himself was punished in body and spirit for six months.

The episode of Bat-sheba was a turning point in David's life. The remaining parts of II Samuel detail his punishment. It is as if pushing down the single domino by raping Bat-sheba and killing her husband and his platoon toppled a long series of other dominos. Five of his children died, as did Uriah and his troopers whom he had murdered: the child of his union with Bat-sheba, his daughter Tamar, and three of his sons Amnon, Absalom, and Adonijah. Amnon raped his half-sister Tamar and was killed by her brother Absalom. Absalom rebelled against his father David, as David rebelled against the trust that Uriah placed in him, and David had to run for his life. Absalom bedded David's concubines, as he bedded Bat-sheba.

---

3. Nathan appears to David three times in the books of Samuel and Kings. The appearances can be interpreted as three critiques of David's rule. The first is when Nathan informs David that he and his descendants will reign over Israel forever, but also tells him that he cannot build a temple to God (II Samuel 7). Why? Nathan, Solomon, and the book of Chronicles give three different answers. However, it is also possible that Nathan recalled how David assumed certain priestly functions in II Samuel 6, and was, in effect, telling David that the ruler of Israel cannot also be its spiritual leader. Here, Nathan is criticizing David for thinking that as a ruler he is above the law. In I Kings 1, he informs David that a ruler must indicate who will rule after him, and not focus only on himself and be satisfied to have ruled well.

David's son Adonijah tried to bed David's last concubine and was killed by Solomon. Sex was involved in each affair.

Is David punished *midah keneged midah*, "measure for measure," punished in the same manner that he acted, "tit for tat"? David ordered the death of one person and five of his children were killed. He ravished one woman and many of his concubines were similarly treated. An answer is possible. First, it should be recalled that David also caused the death of many soldiers in the way he had Uriah killed. Second, he tried four times to send Uriah to his wife, and four of his sons were killed. Third, although David's son Absalom ravished many concubines, it was all part of a single act, one act of outrage equal to the outrage that David visited upon Uriah and Bat-sheba. Also, arguably, the bedding of David's concubines had to be many concubines to parallel his misdeed because David had many wives and concubines – where Uriah had but one wife – and the violation of one concubine would not have afflicted him as he had afflicted Uriah. Thus, one could see David's punishment as tit for tat.

David acknowledged that his acts were wrong and repented, but none of the punishments were lessened. And this raises the question: Is repentance designed to erase crimes?

THE TALMUD, LOVING DAVID, INSISTS HE COMMITTED NO CRIME

Contrary to the plain reading of the chapters, the Babylonian Talmud, *Shabbat* 56a, states that David did no wrong. It offers various reasons why David acted properly, including that Bat-sheba and Uriah were divorced and that Uriah deserved death because he did not obey David's order to go home.

Others recognize that David acted improperly. Don Isaac Abarbanel states that the text itself says that David did wrong and asks how the Talmud can say that David did no wrong. Abarbanel tries to justify the Talmud in a manner many would find unsatisfactory. He writes,[4] "Since he repented and received his punishment, with this [punishment] his wrong was erased."

SHOULDN'T REPENTANCE ABSOLVE DAVID OF HIS WRONGDOING?

Why was David punished? He repented. Shouldn't his act be forgiven? This story

---

4. Abarbanel, *Perush Abarbanel*.

shows that acts are not wiped clean even when a person regrets the misdeed. The message is repeated frequently in Scripture. The concept of repentance did not exist during the days when the book of Samuel was written. At that time, people believed that acts are like eggs: once an egg is cracked, it is impossible to reassemble the cracked pieces. In other words, the ancients saw behavior in a natural way: one cannot make a misdeed disappear by saying words.

This was also the view of Maimonides: wrong action had to be corrected by proper actions.[5] Maimonides believed that God's involvement in the world is limited to the laws of nature; all occurrences are outcomes of natural causes, not God's direct involvement.[6]

This concept can be extended to the question of punishment. Rather than being punishments, natural consequences of misdeeds can often be mistaken for retribution. The sages explain that *aveirah goreret aveira*, one misdeed causes another misdeed: there are natural consequences to acts, which come despite regret.[7] Other cultures recognized this fact as well.

THE MYTH OF HERCULES

The educated Greeks and Romans understood the Greek and Roman myths as parables, as the Greek philosopher Plato states explicitly in several of his philosophical works. The myths teach important moral lessons to the masses who could not be taught by a more direct method. The myth of Hercules is one such myth, and relevant to our discussion.

Hercules was his Roman name, but in the original Greek version he was called Heracles, meaning Hera's glory. Hera was the wife of the Greek God Zeus who fathered Heracles with a mortal woman. Heracles' mother tried to hide the fact of his birth from the goddess Hera by naming her child after her. The trick did not work, of course, because the gods cannot be fooled, and, in any event, any

---

5. As I wrote elsewhere, if one slaps his wife and later comes home and asks his wife why she is still angry, "You shouldn't be angry. I went to the synagogue and did repentance," is clearly absurd.

6. Maimonides, *Guide of the Perplexed*, 2:48.

7. Once we accept this premise, other answers fall into place. For one, critics argue that Nathan's prophecy was probably invented and written after the event because a human being cannot know the future. But, based on our understanding of the episode, consequences flow from deeds, both good from good and bad from bad. It is logical to assume that Nathan knew this and was saying to the king that consequences should be expected to mirror his acts.

woman would remember whether she bore a child, and Hera sought revenge by making Heracles' life miserable.

Heracles was a very strong man. One day he went mad and unintentionally used his strength to kill his wife and children. When his sanity returned he wept copiously and repented his deed. He attempted suicide, but Hera would not leave him be. She stopped the suicide attempt and sent Heracles to Delphi. At Delphi, Apollo's oracle told him that his crime would be discharged if he served the king of Tiryns slavishly for a year, performing twelve tasks, and then served a queen in Asia for a year. At the end of the story, Heracles completed the tasks and married again, only to be killed by his new wife, who mistakenly gave him a coat laced with a poison lotion that she was given during one of Heracles' heroic acts, for she thought the lotion promoted love and did not kill.

The tale can be interpreted as follows. Heracles, the son of god, was like all people, for all humans are God's creations. Hera can be seen as representing the laws of nature. Heracles committed a gross misdeed, even though it was unintentional, and tried to remove his guilt by penitence and by killing himself. But, as we pointed out, these acts do not erase the consequences of a deed. His madness was irrelevant because, sane or not, he had committed the deed, and his repentance also could not erase the foul act. Although Heracles tried to avoid the punishment for the murder of his wife and children by good behavior, he suffered the consequence of his malicious deed by having to perform many slavish activities, and the ultimate consequence was that his second wife killed him with poison that he himself made available by one of these activities.

In short, the Greek myth teaches the moral that deeds have consequences that may appear to be punishments but are nevertheless natural aftermaths of the acts committed.

This lesson is repeated in many other Greek and Roman myths. In the tale of King Agamemnon, who sacrificed his daughter Iphigenia by the demand of the goddess Artemis and repented his deed, the king was killed by his wife for his barbarous murder despite the fact that he killed his daughter by divine command.[8]

---

8. There is another interesting version of the ending of this tale. The hero Odysseus, like an angel from heaven, sprang forward and cut Iphigenia loose. At that moment a deer trotted out of a bush into the clearing and nuzzled Odysseus. Odysseus cried out: "The goddess wants the deer, not the maiden." And so he saved Iphigenia in a way that closely resembles the story of

Perseus, who accidentally killed his father when he threw a disc, was banished from his country even though his father's death was clearly an accident that he regretted.

There are also many talmudic statements indicating that repentance cannot remove natural consequences.

WHY DIDN'T DAVID LOSE HIS KINGDOM?

Why was Saul punished for his misdeed by losing his kingdom (1 Samuel 15:24), which was given to David, while David did not lose his kingdom? Saul's act showed his inability to act as a king, while David's improper behavior showed a personal flaw. Moses also lost his ability to lead the Israelites because he showed that he was no longer able to lead them when he allowed the people to provoke him, lost his temper, and hit a rock.[9]

---

the binding of Isaac by his father Abraham in Genesis 22. Iphigenia did not die, but went to live in a cloister. It is also interesting that the two versions of the Agamemnon story parallel the two interpretations of the Jephthah story in Judges 11–12. Jephthah vowed to sacrifice the first thing that greeted him when he returned home from war. His daughter greeted him. One version is that he sacrificed her as he vowed. The other is that his daughter cloistered herself for the rest of her life.

9. There are interpretations that state that God told Moses to take his staff with him and hit the rock. There are two versions of Moses and the rock. Some understand that the same story is told twice. In one, the Torah states that God said hit the rock.

PART 5
Absalom vs. David

Chapters 13–19 deal with Absalom's rebellion against his father David, what caused it, and David's failures to address the problems that prompted it. The story should be seen as the consequences that followed David's taking Bath-sheba from her husband Uriah and his murder of Uriah. It confirms the prophet Nathan's prediction.

The story is not in Chronicles probably because it reflects badly upon David and the author of Chronicles wanted to show David in a favorable light.

The Rape of Tamar

II SAMUEL 13

Chapter 13 relates the rather perplexing tale of Amnon's rape of his half-sister Tamar, their father King David's failure to react to the rape, the murder of Amnon committed in revenge by Tamar's full brother Absalom, and Absalom's flight to avoid punishment. Amnon was David's eldest son, as indicated in II Samuel 3:2, and Absalom was his third son born to David and the daughter of Talmai, king of Geshur, according to 3:3. Chapter 13:1 states explicitly that Tamar was Absalom's sister, although, as we will see, the rabbis in the Talmud and some traditional commentators state she was not exactly his sister.

THE CHAPTER RAISES MANY QUESTIONS

1. Why did David fail to react to the rape of his daughter other than to become angry?
2. How did David's reaction compare to the reaction of Jacob when his daughter Dinah was raped?
3. Did Absalom have a moral right to kill Amnon?
4. Why did Amnon and Absalom use subterfuge?
5. How was Absalom's behavior different than that of Jacob's sons?
6. Did David's failure to act properly regarding Amnon cause Absalom to rebel against his father?
7. Why didn't David require Amnon to marry Tamar, the woman he raped, as required by Deuteronomy 22:29?
8. Why does the Bible fail to reveal what happened to Tamar and Dinah in their later life?

Many commentators have spoken about these questions at length and we will view a few, but not all, of them within the context of our goal to understand what the Bible actually states and to view Scripture in a rational manner.

THE STORY

The story appears to be the fulfillment of the punishment that the prophet Nathan predicted would be inflicted upon David, "the sword shall never depart from your house; because you have despised me [God], and have taken the wife of Uriah the Hittite to be your wife.... I will raise up evil against you out of your own house." The punishment is fulfilled by David's son Amnon raping Tamar and by his death, parallel measure for measure to the taking of Bat-sheba and the death of Uriah. Future chapters will show how the punishment continues.[1]

Amnon lusted after his half-sister Tamar, the sister of Absalom, and pined until he made himself sick. She was a virgin, which, according to Kimchi, inflamed his passion, and according to Rashi reflected the hopelessness of his passion because virgins lived in a secluded area.[2] She was described as wearing a *khutonet passim*, usually translated as a "garment of many colors," the same kind of garment that the patriarch Jacob gave his son Joseph,[3] who he loved more than any other of his children. When Joseph served as a slave in Egypt, his master's wife tried to have sex with him. He ran and left his coat.[4]

His cousin, the son of David's brother who was very wise,[5] suggested that

---

1. The prophecy is also fulfilled by the death of David and Bat-sheba's first child and by the events in the rest of the book of II Samuel. It is unclear whether David raped Bat-sheba. The Bible only tells us that David saw Bat-sheba and ordered his men to bring her to him. No information is given about her reaction. We also do not know why David was so concerned that people discover that he impregnated Bat-sheba that he went so far to cover-up what occurred by ordering the murder of her husband.

2. There is no biblical support for the view that the ancient Israelites secluded virgins.

3. Genesis 37:3, 23.

4. Genesis 39:12. Should we compare the two instances and derive an understanding from these two incidences? Should we compare them with the rape of Dinah in Genesis 34? Both 13:12 and Genesis 34:7 are similar in saying that such a vile deed should not be done in Israel. There are a number of seduction tales in scripture, as in Genesis 19. Should we compare them?

5. David surrounded himself with family, such as his nephews being leaders of his army. Should we understand that Amnon received bad advice from a relative who was probably, but not certainly, on David's staff, as showing how nepotism is bad, that if David's staff were not relatives the situation would have been different. The same question can be asked about David's nephew Joab: If David did not appoint him as his general would he have had less problems and his life have been better.

Amnon persuade Tamar to come to his dwelling and prepare a meal for him, suggesting that his closeness to her would satisfy his desire. Amnon requested his father David to send her to him, and David, fooled as Uriah was fooled, complied. But Amnon is not satisfied with just observing her.[6]

Amnon told Tamar that he wanted to sleep with her and implied that he would not let her leave his bedroom if she did not comply. She tried to stop him by repeating *al*, "no," three times.[7] When he persisted, she tried to dissuade him with several arguments and then, in 13:13, she says: "Now therefore, I pray you, speak to the king [our father David]; for he will not withhold me from you."

Amnon ignores her request, and rapes her.

MORE QUESTIONS

1. Was David's punishment inflicted upon him by a miraculous intervention of God in human affairs?
2. Why should we try to read a biblical narrative as a natural event?
3. How can Tamar suggest that their father will allow Amnon and his half-sister to marry and violate Leviticus 18:9 that forbids such a union?
4. Is there another instance in Genesis where Abraham married his half-sister?
5. Should we construe Tamar's plea to Amnon that they petition David to allow them to marry as a viable possibility?
6. How did the Talmud understand the story and Tamar's request?
7. Why is the talmudic view anachronistic and unlikely?
8. Must an observant Jew accept a talmudic explanation of Scripture that is not feasible?
9. If the talmudic interpretation of the events of chapter 13 is unreasonable, why did Maimonides support the talmudic solution?
10. How did Joseph ibn Caspi and Isaac Abarbanel see the events?

---

6. Another interpretation of the words in the verse is that the cousin actually suggested that Amnon rape her.

7. Three is used in Scripture many times for emphasis. We are reminded of Tamar's refusal in verse 25 where Absalom invites his father David to join the festivities of sheep-shearing, together with all of his brothers. This was a ploy that, unknown to David, to bring his brother Amnon to a place where he can have his men murder him in revenge for the rape. David refuses twice, using the word *al*, "no," the same verbal refusal used by Tamar.

WAS THIS DAVID'S PUNISHMENT?

One could, of course, understand that God interfered with the laws of nature and performed unnatural acts to punish David for his misbehavior with Bat-sheba. This was how Radak understood the narrative. In his commentary to verse 15 that states that Amnon became angry after the rape, Radak writes that God caused Amnon to hate Tamar after he had intercourse with her in order to punish David. This is curious theology, that God will cause two people to be harmed because of David's act.

A simple and reasonable reading of the chapters shows that the events that took place after David's encounter with Bat-sheba followed a natural and not a supernatural course. The chapter starts with the words "And it came to pass after this," which many commentators understand to mean that after David's son Amnon saw the devious immoral tactics of his father to satisfy his desires with Bat-sheba – which appear in the two preceding chapters that also begin with the words "And it came to pass" – he was emboldened to gratify his own desire. Amnon saw how his father used force to acquire Bat-sheba and decided to do the same to satisfy his own sexual desires. He obviously felt that David would find it hard to criticize him for doing what he, David, had done. Similarly, when Absalom decided to take revenge, he also used force. Additionally, in contrast to Radak who contended that God made Amnon angry, Gersonides explains more reasonably that after the rape, when his ardor cooled, Amnon's natural reaction was to become furious at the threats that Tamar had made to him before and during the rape.

THE TALMUD'S UNDERSTANDING OF THE TAMAR TALE

The Babylonian Talmud, *Sanhedrin* 21a, states that King David had four hundred children born as a result of the law in Deuteronomy relating to captive women, discussed below, which would mean that he had relations with far more than four hundred captive women because the law only allows a man to have intercourse once with a captive.[8] "Rav Judah further said in Rav's name, 'Tamar was a daughter of a captive woman, as it is written, "... speak to the king; for he will not withhold me from you." Now should you imagine that she was an offspring of a legitimate marriage, how could a sister have been granted him [in marriage]? We must infer

---

8. The is the view of the talmudic rabbis who were convinced, although there is no proof, that David knew about and observed Moses's Torah.

therefore, that she was the daughter of beautiful captive woman [who, as we will see, is not considered the daughter of the man who bore her].'"

THE VIEW OF MAIMONIDES

Maimonides accepts and explains the talmudic statement. His *Mishneh Torah, Hilkhot Melakhim* 8:1–9 addresses the laws of the captive woman, mentioned in Deuteronomy 21:12. He explains that the Torah allows a soldier who captures a beautiful woman during war, to, in Maimonides' words, "have sexual relations with [the] woman while she is still a non-Jew if his passion overcomes him." However, he may not do so a second time until she decides that she wants to convert and become a Jew, and he must then wait three months before he can marry her and resume having sex. If she does not want to convert, she must be set free.[9]

Then, apropos our situation, in 8:8, Maimonides writes: "If she conceived during the first intercourse [with her captor] the child is a convert. [However] the child is not regarded as [the soldier's] son, because his mother was a non-Jew. The court must immerse him [or her in a ritual bath and convert the child] in their capacity as a court [with authority to do so]. Tamar was [conceived] from [David's] first intercourse with a 'captive woman,' but Absalom was conceived after David married [Tamar's mother]. Thus, Tamar was Absalom's sister only from his mother [but she was not related to David or his son Amnon], and therefore would have been permitted to [marry] Amnon. This is why Tamar said to Amnon 'speak to the king; for he will not withhold me from you.'"

Should we assume that Maimonides considered this Talmudic view the most reasonable way to understand chapter 13? Maimonides, as Saadiah Gaon and ibn Ezra before him and as Gersonides and other rationalists after him, taught that a person is only obligated to accept the rabbinic interpretation of the Bible in respect to *halakhah*, how the rabbis expected a Jew to behave, but not regarding their other statements. If the statement does not conform to reason, the statement, they say, must be interpreted in a way that conforms to reason.

The rabbinical law discussed in the Talmud did not exist in biblical times and therefore could not be the true meaning of the chapter. The Talmud states in essence that the soldier's child from the captive woman is not considered to be

---

9. This view of Maimonides assumes that conversion existed in biblical times, but as shown in my book on Ruth, the concept of conversion did not exist until the second century BCE.

his own child because the child was born of a person who had not converted to Judaism, and once a person converts the convert is considered as if he or she is reborn and the convert's natural parents are not considered his or her parents. In a word, the law is based on the rules of conversion. However, as stated in the prior footnote, conversion did not exist in the biblical period.

Many notable commentators had absolutely no compunction about rejecting the talmudic view as a true report of the event of chapter 13, including Tosaphot, Joseph ibn Caspi and Don Isaac Abarbanel. It is clear, then, that Maimonides only wrote what he did to teach the *halakhah*, not to explain the biblical tale.

THE EXPLANATIONS OF TOSAPHOT, JOSEPH IBN CASPI, AND ISAAC ABARBANEL

Tosaphot state that Tamar was Absalom's sister from another father and was not related to David and Amnon and therefore could marry Amnon. She was called David's daughter, according to Tosaphot, only because she was raised in his house. Tosaphot is rejecting the talmudic tale of Tamar's origin.

Ibn Caspi and Isaac Abarbanel similarly but more expansively note that there is absolutely no indication, not even a hint, of the talmudic history of David having relations with over four hundred beautiful captives, including Tamar's mother, and his siring four hundred children from them. Furthermore, chapter 13 states explicitly and repeatedly that Tamar was Amnon's sister. Therefore, these two commentators explain that Tamar never believed that their father David would condone a marriage between her and her brother. Her intent was only to stop Amnon from raping her, and to stall for time by offering herself in marriage.[10]

AN EVEN SIMPLER EXPLANATION

Once we avoid both halakhic thinking and modern morality, both of which are post-biblical, we will recall that in the biblical period a man could marry his half-sister, as Abraham states in Genesis 20:12, that his wife Sarah "is indeed my sister,

---

10. The Tosaphot were biblical commentators, mostly in France and Germany. The first were relatives of Rashi (1040–1105). The last members lived a couple of centuries after Rashi. Ibn Caspi was a strong fan of Maimonides. He traveled to Egypt to see Maimonides' descendants and was disappointed that they lacked Maimonides' intellect, Abarbanel opposed Maimonides and his rationalism, but was very astute.

the daughter of my father, but not the daughter of my mother; and so she became my wife." Thus it is possible that Tamar's offer to marry Amnon was a legitimate and acceptable one at that time.

SUMMARY

There are quite a few lessons people can learn from this chapter and many questions.

1. One can read chapter 13 as natural events, part of the laws of nature, or as the miraculous interference of God in natural law. David's punishment, foretold by the prophet Nathan, could be seen as natural cause and effect, following his improper act. Amnon saw his father David take a woman forbidden to him, learned from his behavior, and did the same. In contrast, if one sees the events here and in the following chapters as God manipulating people, such as God causing Amnon to become angry, it turns out that God is killing and otherwise hurting innocent people to punish David, which seems wrong.

2. The story serves as another instance where scriptural interpreters attempted to read rabbinical laws anachronistically into a biblical narrative even though the laws did not exist during the biblical period. This backward reading is legitimate and appropriate in regard to teaching *halakhah*, Jewish law, but it is entirely inappropriate when people want to understand the ancient text that they are reading. There are perfectly reasonable explanations for Tamar's assertion that her father David would give her to her brother in marriage. One possibility is that she was agreeing to marry him as permitted in the biblical era, though not in modern times.

3. Reading the Bible without searching for miracles and without applying *halakhah* anachronistically not only reveals what the book of Samuel is actually saying, but also makes the narrative more interesting.

4. The Bible is filled with obscure and ambiguous event, leaving it to readers to interpret what they are reading. Failure to see obscurities and ambiguities causes readers to miss the essence of the stories.

5. It is a mistake to think that there is only one interpretation of a biblical event, and there is no need to do so.

6. If we understand that Abraham married his half-sister and Amnon could do the same, why did the law change?

7. We obtain greater and deeper insight into a biblical tale by comparing the event before us with other similar biblical events, such as the reactions of Jacob and David to the rape of their daughters – while both seemed to be energetic and active before the rapes they appear generally passive for the rest of their lives after the rapes, Joseph's and Tamar's coats of many colors which are torn, Jacob's and Amnon's and Absalom's and David's use of subterfuge, the many rapes in the Bible such as in Judges 21, David's rebellion against his father-in-law Saul and Absalom's rebellion against his father David, and more.

8. We need to recognize the multitude of times that the Bible uses three, and what it indicates when it is used.

9. Despite the rabbis saying that courts of law existed in Israel as early as the days of Moses, saying, for example, that the 70 advisors that Moses had was a 71 member Sanhedrin, David did not refer Tamar's rape case and Absalom's murder case to a court. Why?

10. Why didn't David mourn the death of Amnon? Should we compare this behavior to his reaction when his and Bat-sheba's child was sick? At that time, David mourned by falling on the floor, but as soon as the child died, he ceased mourning perhaps because there was nothing else he felt he could do. If so, isn't this inconsistent with his mourning the death of all his children by falling on the floor when he is mistakenly told that Absalom killed them all?

11. Why doesn't Scripture tell us what happened to the two rape victims Dinah and Tamar, and is obscure in relating what occurred to Jephthah's daughter in Judges 11?

12. In my book *Who was the Biblical Prophet Samuel?* I pointed out over thirty instances where the author of the approximately 200 verses dealing with Samuel seems not to have known about the Pentateuch, the Torah of Moses, and the people in the book violated Torah law without the narrator commenting on this fact, I will list many more in the Afterword. In this chapter David does not require Amnon to marry Tamar as required by Deuteronomy 22:28, 29. Also, verse 13:13 seems to say that a man may marry his half-sister, while Leviticus 18:9 forbids such a marriage.

Joab Tries To Help Absalom

II SAMUEL 14

Absalom, David's son, ran from his father and country after killing his brother Amnon for raping his sister Tamar. Joab, David's general, saw that David was pining for Absalom after a three-year absence. Under Joab's instigation, a wise woman,[11] a widow from Tekoa,[12] appeared before David with a tale of murder and revenge, pleading for help. She said that one of her sons had killed another and that her family[13] was demanding that she produce the murderer so that they could kill him. As neither of her sons had children, she explained to David that if her second son were killed she would be left without any heirs. She requested that David save her son from the family members who wanted revenge or justice, or something else.[14] David assured her that her son would not be killed. She then told David, in essence, that by not calling Absalom home, he was like the family members who wanted to kill the second son. David got her point and

---

11. Maimonides, *Guide of the Perplexed*, 3:54, defines *chokhmah*, "wisdom," in four ways: (1) knowledge of truths that lead to the knowledge of God, (2) knowledge of workmanship, (3) the acquisition of moral principles, and (4) cunning and subtlety, as in Exodus 1:10 when Pharaoh says about the Israelites "Come on, let us deal wisely with them," in Jeremiah 4:22 "They are wise to do evil," and here with the widow of Tekoa.

12. Ehrlich explains that Scripture mentions the wise woman's city, which was not very close to Jerusalem, because if the woman was from Jerusalem, David would not have made a promise to correct the situation, he would have immediately called the family of the dead man to him and resolved the matter.

13. Verse 7 states that "the whole family" rose up against her; another of a multitude of examples of biblical hyperbole. Verse 16, has the woman asking David to deliver her out of "the hand of the man (singular) that would destroy me and my son together."

14. As usual, and as we will see below, Scripture frequently does not explain why an action is contemplated or taken. It is possible, as Kimchi states, that the relatives wanted the second son killed because women did not inherit in those days, and since there were no other sons, the closest relative would inherit the property of the two dead sons.

instructed Joab to tell Absalom to return home. However, David refused to see Absalom for two years.[15]

QUESTIONS

1. Why did Absalom feel he had to run from his father?
2. Why did Joab try to help Absalom?
3. In the parable, why wasn't the murderer brought to court?
4. What right did the family of the deceased have to kill the murderer?
5. Since, according to his mother, one son killed his brother, what right did David have in assuring her that the murderer would not be punished?
6. What other two biblical examples exist where one brother kills another and neither has children or siblings?
7. How should the two examples be interpreted?
8. Was Absalom under house arrest when he returned to Israel?

WHAT PROMPTED ABSALOM TO RUN?

Why did Absalom fear his father? Surely David would understand that Amnon did wrong in raping his sister, David's daughter.

The text does not reveal why he ran, and we do not know. Perhaps (1) Absalom knew that Amnon was David's first-born son and as such was loved more than his other children. (2) He knew that David most likely expected Amnon to be king after him. (3) He saw that David didn't punish Amnon for the rape of Tamar, possibly because of Amnon's special status as the future king. (4) He may have felt that he lacked status because he was the son of the daughter of a foreign king. (5) He could have felt that even if David did not have him killed, he would not treat him well, and he would receive better treatment in his grandfather's kingdom. Or, perhaps, (6) he feared that David would have him killed.

---

15. The rabbis teach that just as God is merciful, so humans should also be merciful, but David was not (A.F. Kirkpatrick, *Samuel*, Cambridge Bible). David vacillates: he "ought to have exercised discipline" in regard to Amnon and did not do so. "Now when he might be expected to be indulgent and forgiving, he is unnecessarily hash," and as a result he faced a rebellion by Absalom (Kennedy).

WHY DID JOAB TRY TO HELP ABSALOM?

Again, the book does not answer this question, and we can only guess. It could be (1) that Joab had good feelings about the young man; he liked him. (2) Joab was David's cousin and Absalom was related to him, and this may have heightened his feeling for him. (3) Perhaps he wanted to ingratiate himself with Absalom whom he felt certain would succeed David as king. While Absalom was David's third son, we will see in the next chapter that Absalom rebelled against David and asserted he is king. Commentators suppose that David's second son had died and Absalom was in line to succeed his father. (4) It could be that Joab liked David so much that he did not want to see him moping for his son. (5) He also could have been worried that David was still angry at him for killing Abner, and if he could get the king in the mood to forgive Absalom, he would forgive him as well.

WHY WAS THERE NO COURT TRIAL IN THE CASE
OF THE WOMAN FROM TEKOA?

Many rabbinical laws or rules are considered part of what is called *Torah shebal pe.* the oral Torah or oral law, and are not specifically stated in the Bible. Some people are convinced that these laws were revealed at Sinai and that they were observed in the biblical period. Others who accept the idea that God revealed the Torah are equally convinced that Israelite leaders were given the right in the Torah itself to make changes because of new social and economic conditions.[16] Sometime around 200 BCE their changes began to be called the oral law.[17]

People who believe that the rabbinical oral laws were in effect in biblical times are bothered by the absence of a judicial enquiry into the killing of the Tekoa woman's son and the threat of a family member to kill the murderer. This is contrary to the rabbinical understanding of Scripture that requires a judicial proceeding.

Don Isaac Abarbanel offers a solution to the problem. He states that the

---

16. This is explained in my books *Mysteries of Judaism* and *Mysteries of Judaism II.* The books show that even Moses made changes and even Maimonides felt that changes need to be made.
17. It was likely that around this time people began to notice that what they were told is contrary to what is stated in the Torah. They received an answer that God also gave an oral Torah which told how the Torah words should be understood. Those who responded in this way did not want the people to think that they made changes in what God dictated. For example, the punishment "an eye for an eye" meant under the oral law that the culprit had to pay monetary compensation.

mother was requesting that the king use his royal power to preempt the court.[18] This reading resolves the question and maintains that a court existed at the time as required by the oral law. However, the view is problematic in that there is no hint in the story that a judicial proceeding was contemplated, and the mother expresses her fear that her family is about to execute her son.[19]

Earlier, Rabbi Yeshayahu of Terani (c.1165–1240) offered a different idea.[20] He stated that despite the oral law, which he felt was in effect at that time, the court could not adjudicate this specific case because there were no witnesses and the murderer had not been warned not to commit the murder. The second requirement is mandated by oral rabbinical law. This solution is also problematical because even if the court could not adjudicate the case, it must, according to rabbinical law, hear the case and determine if there were witnesses and if the murderer was warned, and there is no mention in the text of a judicial proceeding.[21]

KILLING BY THE FAMILY

The killing of the murderer by family members is also inconsistent with rabbinic requirements. When a murder is committed, Numbers 35:19 gives a close relative the right to kill the murderer under certain conditions. However, the rabbis understand 35:12 to require a judicial determination if those conditions exist; as previously noted, there was no judicial determination here.

---

18. Contrary to the thought of many that Judaism does not give a king more power than a court.

19. There are dozens of biblical events that are contrary to the oral law and those who insist that the oral law was divine and given at Sinai claim that each event required ignoring the oral law because of *horaat shaah*, the exigencies of the time. Needless to say, *horaat shaah* is not mentioned in the Torah. See the excursus that discusses this issue.

20. Rabbi Yeshayahu of Terani is known for stating that he recognizes that the scholars that preceded him were more knowledgeable than him, but he is like a dwarf standing on the shoulders of giants. This idea apparently originated with Bernard of Chartres, who died sometime after 1124, before the birth of Rabbi Yeshayahu. Bernard was comparing the scholars of his age (dwarves) to the scholars of Greece and Rome (giants). This notion of the decline of intelligence is a fundamental view of many Jews and the basis for their reluctance to deviate from past rabbinical decisions, but Maimonides and modern science reject it. See Israel Drazin, *Maimonides: The Exceptional Mind* (Jerusalem: Gefen Publishing House, 2008), chapter 3.

21. Some scholars consider Rabbi Yeshayahu a biblical commentator who seeks the plain meaning of the scriptural text. It is both interesting and instructive to compare his reading of the chapter with that of Abarbanel and Ehrlich and to ask oneself whose interpretation is closer to the wording of the chapter.

In short, it appears that chapter 14 is describing a situation in which King David is a participant in a proceeding that violates rabbinical law. This is not problematic for those who understand that rabbinical law did not exist during David's reign.

UNDER WHAT LAW WAS DAVID ADJUDICATING THE TEKOA WOMAN'S CASE?

It frequently happens that unusual – even seemingly absurd – biblical interpretations can cause intelligent thought. Arnold B. Ehrlich's understanding of II Samuel 14 is a case in point.[22]

Ehrlich has his own unique notion of the law of the time. He argues that in ancient times a man could not be killed for murdering his brother if the murderer had no other siblings and the two brothers had no children. He discusses three instances in the Bible where he reads this rule, and sees it applied in two of the three cases. The first is Genesis 4:15. In his opinion, God followed this rule and did not kill Cain for murdering his brother Abel since there were no siblings and neither had children at the time of the murder.

The second is Genesis 27:45. After Jacob took the blessing that Isaac intended to give to Esau, their mother Rebecca feared that Esau would kill Jacob. She urged Jacob to flee the country. "Why," she said, "should I be bereaved of you both in one day?" There are many different views as to whom "you both" refers.[23] Ehrlich understands that Rebecca feared that Esau would kill Jacob and Jacob's relatives would avenge his death by killing Esau. Since, in contrast to the Cain and Abel story, this story allows the killing of a person who murdered his brother, and seems to contradict his theory. Ehrlich recognizes this and contends that this story of Jacob and Esau must have been written during a later period when the ancient rule had changed.[24]

However, this rather unusual rule still existed during the time of the wise woman of Tekoa for she was arguing, according to Ehrlich, that since she was a widow, had only one son left, and had no grandchildren, King David must order the family to obey this ancient law and desist from seeking revenge.

22. Ehrlich, *Mikra Kipheshuto*, 17, 79, and 222.
23. Rashi and Radak understand Rebecca to be referring to Jacob's sons, ibn Ezra interprets that each will kill the other, and Chazkuni believes that the two people are Isaac and Jacob because Esau said he would kill Jacob when Isaac died. As in the previous note, we can ask again which of these commentators is closest to the plain meaning of the text and why.
24. Ehrlich felt that the biblical tale of Jacob and Esau was composed after the reign of King David.

WAS ABSALOM UNDER HOUSE ARREST WHEN HE RETURNED TO ISRAEL?

It seems that David did not act wisely. By bringing Absalom home, but refusing to see him for two years, and possibly even placing him under house arrest, he "did not save the second son." David placed him in a worse condition than he was in when he was in his grandfather's kingdom.

What prompted some commentators to think that Absalom was under house arrest? Verse 29 states that Absalom sent for Joab to complain that his father refused to see him. It may be that he had to send for Joab because he was not allowed to leave his home. However, it is also possible that after seeing his father ignore him for a total of five years, he decided to rebel and began to act as his father's successor, and "summoned" Joab.

Joab went to David and pleaded Absalom's case. David called Absalom to him and kissed him.[25] But it was too late. Absalom wanted revenge.

---

25. Ehrlich explains that the text does not reveal what David said to his son, for there was no need to state it. The kiss said all that needs to be said, that David forgave his son. Similarly, when Esau kissed Jacob when he returned after a twenty-year absence, when Jacob fled lest Esau kill him for stealing the blessing of their father which Isaac intended to give to Esau, the kiss in Genesis 33:4 indicates that Esau forgave his brother. It does not state there that Jacob kissed Esau because there was nothing for Jacob to forgive.

The Ironic Tale of Ahithophel

II SAMUEL 15

Some biblical tales were written as humorous, misdirecting irony; often, the literal reading of these stories is the opposite of the irony that was intended. Many examples of this phenomenon exist. A good example is the story of Ahithophel related in II Samuel 15–17. Ahithophel served as an advisor to King David, but when David's son Absalom rebelled against him, Ahithophel switched sides and joined Absalom as his advisor. The Bible repeatedly characterizes Ahithophel as a wise man, sometimes overstating the description. In 16:23, the Bible writes: "Now the counsel of Ahithophel which he counseled in those days was as if a man inquired of the word of the Lord; so was the counsel of Ahithophel both with David and with Absalom." Was Ahithophel really wise, or is this biblical irony?[26]

WHO WAS AHITHOPHEL?

The Bible reveals no facts about Ahithophel; even the meaning of his name is obscure. The author of Samuel may have hidden his origin because it is irrelevant to his story. Or perhaps the name itself is ironic.

The letters *Ah* of his name mean "brother." The word *thophel* can mean "tasteless, unseasoned, without merit, and unseemly." Perhaps – and this is only conjecture – the name implies that its owner was not really wise at all. Perhaps the name is hinting at the irony of the story.

Names in the Bible may originate in one of three ways. Parents may have given the child the name at birth to describe some family event or an occurrence at birth. Examples include the names given to the children of Jacob. Second, an explanation of an already existing name may have been invented when the child achieved

---

26. The question will be asked about Solomon in my next book.

maturity, as a kind of *derasha*, an imaginative way of describing the person. For example, Esau might have complained that Jacob was named properly because his name refers to a heel and Esau complains that "he continually tries to grab me by my heels and defeat me." If we accept the explanation of Ahithophel's name as one who is not wise, it is no more than a *derasha*, sermonic. A third possibility, if one rejects the authenticity of the biblical account, the names may have been invented by the narrator to describe the character of his creation.[27]

In any event, while the Bible described Ahithophel's political mind, the rabbis went further and stated that he was also well versed in Torah and taught David religious teachings.[28] The rabbis may have been heightening the irony in the text and saying that despite his wisdom and Torah learning, Ahithophel was not able to use his wisdom against the king chosen by God.

Some scholars identify Ahithophel as the grandfather of Bat-sheba, whom David took as his wife after having her husband killed.[29] There is no way of proving this conjecture. These scholars suggest that Ahithophel was angered by David's behavior with his granddaughter and his desire for revenge led him to join Absalom's rebellion. In any event, this is not a crucial fact in understanding the narrative of chapters 15–17.

ABSALOM'S REBELLION

Absalom used every opportunity to ingratiate himself with the people. Then, "it came to pass at the end of forty years"[30] that Absalom requested permission from his father to go to Hebron to offer sacrifices there. No reason is given for his choosing this city. He went to Hebron with an escort of fifty men who ran before him.[31]

---

27. David is based on a word meaning "beloved," and Solomon on a word meaning "peace."
28. *Pirkei Avot* 6, *Seder Eliyahu Zutta* 17, *Kallah Rabbati* 8, Babylonian Talmud, *Sukkah* 53b, and Jerusalem Talmud, *Sanhedrin* 10, 2. One of the lessons attributed to him was that people learn more when they study with another than when they study alone.
29. These scholars identify the Ahithophel here with the man of the same name in 23:34.
30. 15:7.
31. 15:1. Later, in 1 Kings, when Adonijah wanted to make himself king, he also had fifty men run before him. While it is clear that the escort was to show that he would be king, the significance of the fifty is obscure.

WHY DID ABSALOM CHOOSE HEBRON?

Absalom may have told his father that he wanted to travel to the city where the patriarchs were buried and make a sacrifice upon an altar there. Yet, his plan was to proclaim himself king in Hebron. Why did he choose this city? We can only guess, because Scripture does not address the issue. It may be: (1) His choice was to announce that he was now the king in the city where David had been proclaimed king. (2) Hebron was considered a holy city in those days, as it is today for many Jews, and sacrifices were offered to God from this city, and the city would add some sanctity to his announcement. (3) Hebron was the city of Absalom's birth and he had many friends there (Ehrlich). (4) David's core constituency was from his tribe Judah, and Absalom wanted to start his rebellion by stealing their alliance from David. (5) Judah had always stood separate from the other tribes, as hinted as early as Genesis 38, Judah's confrontation with Joseph in Genesis 44, and in the actions of the tribe in the books of Joshua and Judges. Absalom felt that the tribe had always felt it was not part of Israel and a good start was to draw the tribe to him. (6) He may have seen that Judah was not happy that their king, a man who could make them rich and happy, left them to rule over the united tribes (Ehrlich). (7) While sacrifices needed to be brought in a holy city and Jerusalem was a holy city, people have more respect for something, someone, or some place that is distant than for what is near. David would understand that Absalom would choose a holy city which was far away (Ehrlich).[32]

When Absalom reached Hebron, he started his rebellion by declaring himself king. He sent for Ahithophel, who joined him willingly.

FORTY YEARS

The statement that these events occurred after "forty years" is problematic. What does it mean? The Septuagint, Peshitta, Vulgate,[33] and Josephus read "four years."

---

32. Maimonides, whom Ehrlich does not mention here, uses this insight to explain the laws of impurity. In his *Guide of the Perplexed* 3:49, he states that here is nothing impure about touching a dead body or the other items that make a person "impure." The Torah wanted to restrict the times that people visit the temple. If people visit it often, they will lose their feeling that the temple is a place of sanctity. The Torah invented the notion of "impurity" to keep the people away from the temple on many occasions so that they will like it better when they are allowed to attend.
33. The Peshitta, meaning "simple" (suggesting that it is the plain meaning of Scripture), is an Aramaic translation of the Bible by an unknown author or authors that was composed in the

"Forty," according to these sources, Ehrlich and many other commentators, is a scribal error, with the original having "four," presumably four years after the reconciliation between Absalom and his father just mentioned in chapter 14. Other solutions have been offered, including forty years since the first king Saul was appointed king of Israel or the forty years refers to the last year of David's reign, when he was 70 years old and would soon die. Since Absalom may have heard that David promised his kingdom to his younger brother Solomon, Absalom may have realized that this was a necessary and opportune time for him to seize the kingdom.

DAVID'S REACTION

This view would explain David's unusual behavior. David fled and left his concubines behind.[34] Why? He had always been an active man of war. He had always shown interest in women. Why did he behave differently now? No reason is given. If we realize: (1) Many years had passed since David fought wars and that he was now old and weak, his behavior is understandable. (2) David may have lost his courage. (3) It is also possible that David retreated because he did not want to battle his son Absalom who he had come to love. (We see later how he mourned Absalom's death.) He may have thought that if he left Jerusalem, an opportunity would arise where he could return with full power without harming his son.

Yet, despite his physical weakness or his love for his son, David planned his retreat wisely. All the while displaying signs of mourning,[35] he had the presence

---

first half of the first millennium. Most scholars believe that it was composed for the Christian community, although it renders the Pentateuch very similar to the rabbinically sanctioned Targum Onkelos. The Vulgate is a Latin translation of the Bible composed by Jerome in the fifth century. "Vulgate," as the word "vulgar," refers to the common people and reveals that the Vulgate, like the Peshitta and Targum Onkelos, was composed for the average man.

34. 15:16 states that David left behind ten concubines "to keep the house." It is unclear what he expected these women to do. They certainly were unable to protect the house from seizure and themselves from rape. Arnold Ehrlich explains that men during David's time had three kinds of women: wives, concubines, and slaves. Wives were the most trustworthy of the three and slaves the least. So David, who did not want to leave his wives for Absalom to mistreat, and did not trust his slaves, had to leave his concubines to do whatever they could do. It is also possible that David did not think that Absalom would stoop so low as to rape his concubines.

35. Ehrlich notes that David displayed signs of mourning in this chapter when he heard of Absalom's rebellion. He asks why bathing is forbidden during a time of mourning. What does it have

of mind to instruct some supporters to remain in Jerusalem to keep him informed of Absalom's plans.

WHY DID DAVID INSTRUCT HIS PEOPLE TO TAKE THE ARK BACK TO JERUSALEM?

When David began his retreat, he took the ark of God with him. The people at that time felt that God was somehow associated with the ark and having the ark with them in battles, for example, would assure divine help.[36] Yet, after starting his retreat, David told two young priests to take the ark back to Jerusalem. Why? It appears that David was not as superstitious about the ark as the general population. He felt that a good tactic would be to have people he trusted living in Jerusalem who could report to him what Absalom was doing so that he could take advantage of the situation if the opportunity arose. As priests, the two young men would have many chances to hear and see what Absalom and his forces were doing.

Similarly, when one of his elderly advisors, Hushai the Archite,[37] requested that David allow him to accompany him during the retreat, David told him that Hushai would serve him better by making Absalom believe that he wanted to be Absalom's advisor, as he was for his father. While being with Absalom, he could give him bad advice. This tactic worked. The three men brought David the kind of information he needed.

AHITHOPHEL'S FIRST ADVICE TO ABSALOM

Ahithophel, who had been one of David's advisors abandoned David and joined

---

to do with mourning? Why is it different, for example, from washing one's hands or brushing one's teeth, which are not proscribed?

He states that our current bathing practices differ from those of the past. We bathe frequently, many even daily, because we see bathing as a hygienic necessity and a necessity to avoid social embarrassment. The ancients, he states, did not see it this way. They thought of bathing as a luxury that a person would indulge in at times of leisure. Since the people saw bathing as a luxury and since people should not engage in luxurious activities while mourning, bathing was forbidden.

36. This was pure superstition and did not assure victories, as when the Israelites fought against the Philistines in 1 Samuel 4, the Israelites were defeated, the priests who brought the ark were killed, and the Philistines took the ark to their country.

37. The "Archite" refers to his family (Segal, Kiel, and others).

Absalom and gave him guidance. What was Ahithophel's first suggestion to Absalom? In 16:22–23,

> Ahithophel said to Absalom: "Go unto your father's concubines, that he left to keep his house; and all Israel will hear that you despise your father; and the hands of all that are with you will be strong." So they spread Absalom a tent upon the top of the house; and Absalom went unto his father's concubines in the sight of all Israel.

It is at this point, in verse 24, that the Bible highlights the irony by repeating the word "counsel" three times and exaggerating it in comparison to the "word of the Lord":

> Now the counsel of Ahithophel, which he counseled in those days, was as if a man inquired of the word of the Lord; so was the counsel of Ahithophel both with David and with Absalom.

DID THE ADVICE BRING THE DESIRED RESULTS?

Scholars relate that pagans showed that they had assumed the dynasty of a prior king by taking his wives. Thus, Ahithophel was suggesting to Absalom that he make a demonstration to the people that he was now king. Yet there is no indication in the narrative that the people rallied to Absalom after he took his father's concubines as Ahithophel had predicted.

Not only did Ahithophel fail to aid Absalom with this advice, but unbeknownst to him he was, in effect, fulfilling the divine prediction announced by the prophet Nathan in 12:11: "Behold, I will raise up evil against you out of your own house, and I will take your wives before your eyes, and give them to your neighbor, and he will lie with your wives in the sight of the sun."

The biblical author, it would appear, is reflecting the later Yiddish aphorism, *a mench tract und gat lached*, "Man thinks, but God laughs."

AHITHOPHEL'S SECOND ADVICE IN CHAPTER 17

In 17:1, Ahithophel requested:

> Let me now choose out twelve thousand men, and I will arise and pursue after David tonight; and I will come upon him while he is weary and weak-handed,

and will make him afraid; and all the people that are with him will flee; and I will smite the king only; and I will bring back all the people to you; and all will have returned, [except] the man whom you seek, and all the people will be in peace.

Ahithophel's tactic was a surprise nighttime attack. Feeling that David showed weakness when he fled, he assumed that those with David would be passive. But, although the narrative ironically states that he was "wise," Ahithophel was not suggesting a novel idea; this was the same tactic that David had used repeatedly. Additionally, Ahithophel did not count on David's forethought to set spies with Absalom to report his activities. Hushai the Archite, one of these people, suggested a different plan to Absalom and then sent two messengers to warn David of the two plans. Absalom rejected Ahithophel's suggestion and accepted Hushai's idea.

Having his advice rejected saddened Ahithophel. He went home, put his affairs in order, and strangled himself. This may be the greatest irony of the story; it is certainly not the behavior of a wise man.

ANOTHER IRONY IN THE STORY

Ahithophel's first plan was that women, David's concubines, would help Absalom secure his father's kingdom. This, as previously stated, did not work. Additionally, ironically, as in Joshua chapter 2 where a woman hid two Israelite spies and saved them and made Joshua's attack of Jericho successful, the same thing happened here. In chapter 17 of this book a woman hid the two messengers that Hushai sent to David to warn him of an attack, and saved his king from Absalom. Thus, rather than women aiding in the elevation of Absalom, they helped bring him down.

We will see another, even more startling example of irony in chapter 25.

David's Encounters as He Flees Jerusalem

II SAMUEL 16

David has two encounters as he leaves Jerusalem during the rebellion. In one, he is duped. It is brazen humbuggery. In the second, he is insulted, and does not respond to the insult as he did years earlier when Nabal insulted him, when he decided to kill Nabal, and was only appeased when Nabal's wife gave him a huge gift and begged him to reconsider his attack.

ZILBA

First, Zilba the servant of Mephibosheth, the son of Jonathan and grandson of King Saul, meets David and his entourage with refreshing gifts of food and drink, which, unstated in the text, is similar to the gifts that Abigail sent to David in 1 Samuel 25:18 when she tried, successfully, to stop David and his army from taking revenge against her husband for the insult Nabal made against David.[38] David had shown kindness to Mephibosheth by giving him all of the property belonging to King Saul and inviting him to eat at the king's table. Upon seeing Zilba, David asked why Mephibosheth did not join him during his retreat as Zilba did. Zilba said, "Behold, he remained in; for he said: 'Today the house of Israel will restore

---

38. Although David's troops that left Jerusalem must have been far larger than the six hundred soldiers during the time of Abigail, Ziba's gift was smaller. Both gave two hundred loaves, one hundred clusters of raisins, and had them carried on asses. But Zilba only sent one container of wine, compared to two from Abigail. He did not send, as Abigail did, five sheep that were already dressed, five measures of parched corn, and two hundred cakes of figs. He did send one hundred summer fruits that Abigail did not send. Kimchi states that the asses were sent not only to carry the gifts but also for David's wives to ride upon, but while this would indicate that Zilba was considerate, the text does not say that this was his intention.

to me the kingdom of my father.'"[39] David rewarded Zilba for warning him about the turnabout of Mephibosheth's fealty, granting him all of the property that he had previously given Mephibosheth.

In essence, as we will see, Zilba's statement most likely reflected the still existing division between the northern tribes and the tribe of Judah. Judah had always lorded it over the other tribes. Saul of Benjamin led the northern tribes for some years, now David had snatched the throne from the north, and many northerners wanted it restored. This is also what prompted Shimei to act as he did.

But what did Zilba expect to gain personally by his actions. (1) It is possible, but unlikely, that he was telling David the truth, that despite what David did for Mephibosheth, he had bad feelings toward David and wanted him harmed. (2) Zilba may not have expected a gift in return for his gift immediately, but was hedging his bet. He did not know who would survive the rebellion, but he gave David the gifts so that if David survived he would remember what Zilba did and treat him well. (3) He lied hoping for an immediate gift of Mephibosheth's property. (4) He did not fear that if Absalom won, Absalom would take the property from him, because in those days, it was forbidden for a king to take away the property belonging to another, as seen in the story of Ahab and Jezebel.[40] (5) Even if Absalom took the property from him, it was worth the gamble he was taking; he would only loose what he did not have at present, David's gifts.

SHIMEI

Soon thereafter, Shimei, "a man of the family of the house of Saul,"[41] standing on a hill facing the retreating army, cursed David, and threw stones and dust at him. One of David's generals wanted to ascend the hill and kill him but David didn't allow it. He said, "Look, my son who came from my body seeks my life; how much more this Benjamite now? Let him alone, and let him curse; for the Lord has decreed him [to do so]. Perhaps the Lord will see my iniquity, and the Lord will

---

39. Goldman suggests that it is improbable that Mephibosheth would think that he now had a chance to be king and Zilba was lying to David, and David was duped. This should remind us of the Amalekite in chapter 1 who said that he killed Saul. Both said what they said to gain a gift from David.

40. 1 Kings 21. King Ahab wanted property belonging to a man who did not want to sell it to him. Jezebel had to devise a scheme whereby her husband could acquire the land.

41. 16:5. Shimei was a Benjamite, just as Saul.

pay me well for his cursing me today."[42] Later, when David successfully returned to Jerusalem, he did not punish Shimei – but on his deathbed he instructed his son and successor Solomon to do so.[43]

QUESTIONS

1. What would cause Mephibosheth to think that "the house of Israel will restore the kingdom of [his] father" to him?[44] Did he think that Absalom would give up the throne that he was rebelling to conquer?
2. Is there significance to the fact that Shimei was a relative of the late King Saul?
3. Why did David not kill Shimei during the attack or in its aftermath? Why did he tell Solomon to kill him?
4. Why did David mention his son's rebellion in discussing Shimei?
5. Did David really believe that God wanted him to be cursed?
6. Did David truly think that God would reward him for allowing himself to be cursed and stoned?

THE POTENTIAL POLITICAL STORM FACING DAVID

A careful examination of the historical biblical books Joshua, Judges, Samuel, and Kings reveals that Judah stood apart from the other tribes, holding a favorable position from the onset of the conquest of Canaan, and even before. It is likely that Samuel recognized the division between the tribe of Judah and the other tribes and, wanting to unite the twelve tribes, purposely chose the first king, Saul, from the tribe of Benjamin. The choice was seemingly wise. The king was from a non-Judean tribe and satisfied the Israelites. On the other hand, the tribe chosen, Benjamin, was one of the smaller and weaker tribes and, therefore, apparently no

---

42. 16:11 and 12. Ehrlich explains that "for the Lord has decreed it so" is not what David thinks about his relationship with God, but what Shimei thinks: Shimei, who was a Benjamite like Saul, thinks that God is causing all of these difficulties for David because he stole the reign over Israel from Saul's family. Ehrlich comments that David had a right under the law of the time to kill Shimei for cursing him. But it is characteristic of self-centered David to do what is important for himself. Thus, for example, he did not bring the ark to Jerusalem because of the honor of the ark, but for his own honor. So, here, he did not kill Shimei so people would not think he is starting a war with the northern tribes.

43. I Kings 2.

44. 16:3.

threat to Judah. Additionally, Benjamin held land adjacent to Judah and therefore was presumably friendlier to Judah than the other tribes.

This is why David was very careful not to antagonize the non-Judeans when he assumed reign over all the Israelite tribes. For example, he waited years after the death of Saul, years spent in negotiations, before he assumed rule of all the tribes. Furthermore, he moved his capital from Hebron, from where he had ruled over the tribe of Judah, to Jerusalem, which was not in Judean territory, but was near the border between Judah and the other tribes.

Despite Samuel's and his attempts, David knew that the northern tribes were never fully satisfied with his rule, a fact that would prove true when they split from Rehoboam, Solomon's son, and formed their own kingdom. He also knew that at an opportune moment, they would rebel against him. He feared that the northern tribes led by the Benjamites (Saul's tribe) would use the opportunity of Absalom's rebellion, when his kingdom was split and he was weak, to rebel.

DAVID'S UNDERSTANDING OF MEPHIBOSHETH'S PLAN

When David heard that Mephibosheth had said that the house of Israel would return the kingdom to Saul's family, he most likely understood that Mephibosheth did not expect Absalom to give the kingdom to him. Rather, the non-Judean tribes, would take advantage of the split in David's kingdom, attack, and seize Absalom's kingdom for Saul's grandson.

THE SIGNIFICANCE OF SHIMEI

It was with these thoughts in mind that David encountered Shimei, a member of Saul's family.

David mentioned his son's rebellion because he knew that the non-Judean tribes would utilize it as their opportunity to usurp the kingdom. He also knew that if he killed Shimei, his death would make him into a martyr and be the spark to ignite the rebellion. The non-Judeans would overlook Shimei's behavior and the fact that David was provoked. Even after David returned to his capital, he knew that he was still not secure from a tribal attack, as shown in chapter 20, when Sheba, another Benjamite, rebelled saying, "'We have no portion in David, neither have we an inheritance in the son of Jesse; every man to his tents, Israel.'

So all the men of Israel[45] went up from following David and followed Sheba the son of Bichri; but the men of Judah did cleave to their king."

As pointed out in the last chapter, these events probably occurred when David was quite old. And so, shortly thereafter, on his death bed, David advised his son to kill Shimei at the appropriate time, when his kingdom was secure, to avoid a future rebellion.

SHIMEI'S CHARGE AGAINST DAVID

Shimei shouts "the Lord returned upon you all the blood of Saul's house."[46] We do not know, because the Bible is silent on this point, precisely what Shimei meant. He could have been referring to what he considered David's complicity in the murders of Saul's and Ish-bosheth's general Abner and Ish-bosheth or what he considered a war between David and Saul and Saul's family, or this is simply an overstatement referring to David's assuming the kingship of the northern tribes.

GOD'S ROLE IN THE STORY

Maimonides, as we know, wrote in his *Guide of the Perplexed* 2:48 that humans perform acts that the Bible assigns to God, that God is not involved, and that these acts are under total human control or are the results of nature, not miracles, but are ascribed to God to remind the Bible's readers that God is the ultimate cause of everything because God created the world.

Thus when David seemingly stated that God bade Shimei to curse and stone him, he meant that it was natural and understandable that Shimei would want to act the way he did because he was of Saul's family.

Similarly, when David said that perhaps God would reward him for restraining himself from taking revenge at this time, he was not speaking about a miraculous and divine reward; rather, he meant that his restraint would suspend a rebellion.

SUMMARY

The incidences in chapter 16 seem to be unrelated and irrelevant until they are understood in the context of the constant struggle between Judah and the other tribes that had existed before and since the conquest of Canaan. Understanding

---

45. This is hyperbole, for "all" did not join Sheba.
46. Verse 8.

this political situation clarifies why there was another rebellion later in chapter 20 and why non-Judean tribes joined the rebellion. They were looking for any opportunity to sever their ties with the Judeans.

This also helps explain why David had to instruct his successor Solomon to take action against Shimei. He himself was politically weak, but once Solomon set a firm basis to his kingdom, he would no longer have to fear the tribal split and could dispose of the danger inherent in Shimei. Or so David thought. Unfortunately, the rivalry between north and south continued for generations and the tribes split during the reign of Rehoboam, David's grandson.[47] And the rivalry continued after the split.

---

47. I Kings 12.

Ahithophel's Bizarre Behavior

II SAMUEL 17

The Torah frequently mentions ancient practices and historical ideas that were later changed and elevated to reflect changed ethical ideals. Maimonides cites sacrifices and the lex talionis, the phrase "an eye for an eye,"[48] as examples. He writes in his Guide of the Perplexed 3:32 that the Torah only "allowed" sacrifices that had become customary to the ancients "to continue" as a "concession" to their primitive notions. He writes in 3:41 that the rabbis explained that an "eye for an eye" should be understood as monetary compensation, not mutilation. Other examples of practices include slavery, discussed in the Bible, which Judaism later discontinued, and the requirement to nullify loans during the Sabbatical year that the rabbis changed, allowing the continuation of the loan to further commerce.[49]

ANOTHER CHANGE

Arnold B. Ehrlich (1848–1919) was a brilliant but iconoclastic rabbi and biblical scholar and the author of *Mikra Kipheshuto*, in which he presented interesting, original, frequently non-traditional Bible interpretations. He was shunned by many when he translated the New Testament into Hebrew.

He suggested that suicide be added to the list of post-biblical rabbinical changes.[50] He based his conclusion on the suicide of Ahithophel related in II Samuel 17:23.

---

48. Leviticus 24:20. The term lex talionis is Latin for "retaliation authorized by law."
49. Israel Drazin, *Mysteries of Judaism II: How the Rabbis and Others Changed Judaism* (Jerusalem: Gefen Publishing House, 2017) explains this concept in detail and gives many examples.
50. Ehrlich, *Mikra Kipheshuto*, 234–235.

QUESTIONS

1. What happened to Ahithophel?
2. What did Ahithophel do before his suicide?
3. How does the Bible describe Ahithophel?
4. How did Ehrlich evaluate the rabbinical view of suicide?
5. Is there support for Ehrlich's idea?
6. Why would Maimonides disagree with Ehrlich?

THE AHITHOPHEL STORY

Chapters 13–19 of II Samuel relate the tragic tale of Absalom, David's son, who rebelled against his father. In chapter 17, Ahithophel, whom Absalom elevated to be his advisor, advises Absalom to attack David immediately, surprising him at night with a division of twelve thousand soldiers; Ahithophel himself would lead the attacking forces.[51] This clever advice seemed wise to Absalom and his senior advisors. It would probably have succeeded, but Absalom, in an over-cautious manner,[52] asked Hushai the Archite for his take on the plan.

Unbeknownst to Absalom, Hushai was loyal to David. Hushai argued that Ahithophel's plan failed to take into account David's past exploits. He asserted that David was accustomed to surprise attacks, which he used frequently, and would be prepared for one, easily defeating Absalom's army of twelve thousand. He advised Absalom to wait a short time and gather a larger force from all over Israel for the battle. He added that Absalom should lead the forces himself.

Absalom accepted Hushai's plan over Ahithophel's more reasonable one; the idea that he should lead the military and assume the glory suited his vanity,[53] and

---

51. Presumably, Ahithophel was advising Absalom to recruit a thousand men from each of the twelve tribes, as Moses did in Numbers 31:3–5 in his battle against Midian. Interestingly, a division in the modern American army is approximately the same number, twelve thousand. It is likely that both Ahithophel and Hushai advised Absalom to secure soldiers from every tribe for psychological reasons. Once the tribes committed themselves to fight for Absalom they would begin to feel an increased attachment and commitment to Absalom.
52. Absalom also displayed this same negative trait – over-cautiousness – when he waited a long time before killing Amnon for raping his sister.
53. As shown by Absalom growing his hair long for a vain display. When Absalom fled from the later battle with David's forces, his long hair became entangled in a tree limb, pulled him from his horse, and left him hanging from the tree. He was then captured and killed by one of David's pursuing soldiers.

the delay suggested by Hushai meshed with Absalom's over-cautious tendency to procrastinate and postpone. Hushai's reason for suggesting the delay was that it afforded him time to warn David, preparing him for Absalom's maneuver, a tactic that ultimately worked; David defeated his son's forces. Thus, Absalom's vanity and nature triumphed over Ahithophel's reason. It is also possible that Hushai suggested gathering a large number of soldiers because enlisting so many soldiers would cause much talk and David would thereby be warned of an impending attack.

WHAT HAPPENS TO AHITHOPHEL?

II Samuel does not reveal Ahithophel's thinking following Absalom's rejection of his plan. However, it is reasonable to conclude that he, a seasoned counselor and warrior, foresaw that Absalom was making an enormous error and would be defeated. It is also likely that he knew that when this occurred David would be told of his advice to Absalom and would take revenge by executing him. He must have foreseen that under the law, existing at that time and until the recent past in many countries, the king confiscated the property of a person that he executed. Therefore, since he would surely be killed, he opted to die by a means that saved his property for his family – suicide.

Ahithophel wisely decided to first set his house in order and advise his family how to behave following his death. Although unmentioned in II Samuel, he probably told them not to act antagonistically to David lest he use their antagonism as an excuse to kill them as accomplices to Ahithophel's traitorous advice and seize the property he was leaving them.

A single verse, 17:23, describes Ahithophel's end: "And when Ahithophel saw that his counsel was not followed, he saddled his ass,[54] and arose, and got him home, unto his city, and set his house in order, and strangled himself: and he died and was buried in the sepulcher of his father." This verse does not judge or criticize Ahithophel's suicide.

In chapters 16 and 17 of my *Maimonides and the Biblical Prophets*, four other examples of biblical suicides are examined, demonstrating that there is no explicit

---

54. The phrase "saddled his ass" is also used for Abraham in Genesis 22:3. Both Ahithophel and Abraham were going to a death scene – Abraham to what he understood would be the death of his son Isaac.

biblical prohibition or condemnation of suicide. It was the rabbis who first condemned people who committed suicide.

THE RABBINICAL VIEW

The rabbis interpreted Genesis 9:5, "And surely your blood of your lives will I require; at the hand of every beast will I require it; and at the hand of man, even at the hand of every man's brother, will I require the life of man," to include a prohibition against suicide, even though the plain meaning of the verse does not even hint at this prohibition.[55]

Jewish law today requires that a suicide be buried away from the burial ground of non-suicides, "behind the fence." The early book *Semachot*, composed during the first centuries of the first millennium CE, states that unlike the usual mourning for dead, "There may be no rending of clothes, no baring of shoulders, and no eulogizing for him." The middle practice of baring shoulders is no longer performed for anyone. *Semachot* states that these rules only apply when the suicide was performed *beda'at*, meaning that the suicide knew what he was doing and had control over the situation.

The Bible, as previously stated, did not criticize Ahithophel; indeed, it praised him in 16:3 as being exceptionally wise, and stated that he was buried "in the sepulcher of his father," contrary to rabbinical law for suicides. Thus, Ehrlich seems to be correct in understanding suicide as another example of the rabbis changing biblical law to conform to their ethical beliefs.

EHRLICH'S VIEW ON SUICIDE

Ehrlich asks whether the rabbinical change in the law is reasonable. He argues that the rabbinical enactment is only reasonable when the suicide fails to properly care for his family and society. If suicides leave sufficient funds and property for their spouses to carry on after their death without any burden on the family and with no obligations on society, if the suicides leave no debts, they should, in Ehrlich's opinion, be allowed to do with their bodies body what they will. He claims that the old practice, the biblical practice, is correct and should not have been changed.

This reasoning, he continues, applies to an average individual, one of the vast

---

55. Babylonian Talmud, *Baba Kama* 91b.

majority of humanity, who makes no significant present or future contribution to society. However, it does not apply to a wise person who has the competence to continue to contribute to society's benefit. Wise people rob the community of their future possible contributions by their suicide, and it is wrong for them to kill themselves.

ERRORS IN EHRLICH'S THINKING

Rabbi Solomon ben Abraham Parhon (twelfth century) offered the now generally accepted theological view why the rabbis prohibited suicide: a person's life and body do not belong to him or her but to God, and so people cannot do with their bodies and lives as they please.

This point aside, there are also some practical non-theological reasons for the rabbinical enactment, which Ehrlich did not consider. First, Ehrlich ignores the scientific finding that virtually all suicides are psychologically disturbed and overwhelmed when they kill themselves. It is the rare individual, perhaps Socrates taking the hemlock in 399 BCE, when he could have escaped and saved his life, who is an exception. The rabbis recognized this psychological factor when they said that the mourning rites are not voided for suicides when suicides do not know what they are doing or have lost control over themselves and their circumstances, and they said that the mourning restrictions for suicides are rarely if ever applied. Ehrlich should have also recognized this psychological fact and agreed with the rabbis that no one should be allowed to commit suicide.

Second, even in the possible rare case of a fully unemotional and reasonable suicide, Ehrlich completely overlooked the immediate trauma that a suicide has on his or her family. He did not consider the enduring loss that a family feels over the death of even a "non-productive" family member, their own sense of failure and guilt, as well as the shame that the family feels for years. This is another good reason to prohibit the act.

Third, it is wrong and even arrogant to say that there are people who can make no contribution to humanity.

My father, Rabbi Dr. Nathan Drazin, was a very smart man; among other feats, he knew the Bible by heart. Father asked the question: "Judaism stresses that people should be humble. It also tells us that we should speak truthfully. How is it possible for wise people, who know they are wise, to lie by acting humbly before a person less wise than they know they are?"

Father answered that truly wise people know that they do not know everything[56] and that all other people also possess some knowledge that they do not have. It is therefore not a lie to be humble before everybody. Ehrlich missed this understanding of the value of all people; everyone, not only the wise, has something to contribute to others.

Ehrlich also did not accept Maimonides' final statement in his *Guide of the Perplexed*: humans should strive to develop their intelligence and acquire knowledge and use it to better themselves and society. "Having acquired this knowledge he will then be determined always to seek loving-kindness, judgment, and righteousness."[57]

---

56. We should be reminded of the Socratic paradox: a person's goal is to know him or herself, but wise people know that they do not know everything. Thus, Socrates' wisdom, by his own testimony, was that he did not know.

57. Maimonides, *Guide of the Perplexed* 3:54.

David's Forces Face Absalom

II SAMUEL 18

While Ahithophel commits suicide, Hushai realized that Absalom may come to realize that Ahithophel's plan was better than his plan, and Absalom may not wait to gather a larger army that he would lead. Hushai contacts the priests that David instructed to return to Jerusalem, and tells them to send their sons to David to warn him what both he and Ahithophel had advised Absalom. The two are seen by a lad who reports what he saw to Absalom, and soldiers are sent to find and capture the two spies.

CHASING THE SPIES

What follows is very similar to what transpired to the two spies that Joshua sent to reconnoiter Jericho in Joshua 2: a woman, a maid servant, hid the two youths. As in Joshua, the pursuers asked her where were the two men, and, as there, she said they had left. When they were unable to find them, the pursuers returned to Jerusalem. The two spies then went to David and warned him. David moved his entire troop across the Jordan that night and came to Mahanaim. While there, three rich men, one from Ammon, an Israelite who had cared for Jonathan's son Mephibosheth,[58] and Barzillai an eighty-year-old man, brought beds, vessels, and much food for David and his people, including sheep.[59] David reviewed his troops, organized them, and set commanders over groups of hundreds and thousands.[60]

---

58. Verse 9:4.

59. In 1 Kings 2:7, while on his death bed, David told his son and successor Solomon to treat Barzillai's sons well.

60. Apparently, his force had been augmented by thousands of loyal followers who came to join him (Goldman). According to the Jerusalem Talmud *Rosh Hashanah* 1:1, the rebellion lasted six months.

He divided the troops into three parts. Two were under the command of his cousins Joab and Abishai; the third led by Ittai the Gittite.[61] He arranged for part of his army to remain as a reserve force in Mahanaim to come to the aid of the fighting forces, if needed. He told his armies that he would join them, but seemingly not as a commander. However, the people begged him to remain with the reserve forces.[62] They said that if he came, Absalom's army would focus on killing him. David agreed to remain behind. But before the troops left, David ordered his three commanders in front of the soldiers to go easy "for my sake with the young man, Absalom."

THE BATTLE

David's troops were successful. Some twenty thousand men died that day. Many ran into the forest and more died there than by sword.[63]

Absalom himself encountered David's men and also ran into the forest. Riding so fast, he unheedingly caught his head in the branches of a tree and he hung there as his ass ran away from him.[64]

Why didn't Absalom use his sword to free himself from the tree? The simple answer is that he hadn't the time to do so. He was being pursued, and as soon as he became entangled a soldier found him. Midrashim use events such as this one to teach lessons. Pirkei d'Rabbi Eliezer writes that as he was facing death, Absalom

---

61. Ittai led a force of six hundred and accompanied David when he began his retreat (15:18–22). They were seemingly part of David's non-Israelite mercenary forces from Gath, Philistines, along with other mercenaries, such as the Cherethites and Pelethites. The number six hundred is the exact same number of men in David's army during his early years. This coincidence and that the number six hundred is a round number with six being twice three raises the question of its veracity.

62. The Targum and Rashi suppose the people said, you will help us more by praying for us than leading the army. Abarbanel maintains that while waiting for the results of the battle, he composed Psalm 20.

63. The text does not state if the twenty thousand are just Absalom's men or both his and David's. It also does not disclose how the men died in the forest. The Targum supposes they died from wild beasts. Radak interprets that the twenty thousand were Absalom's men who were punished by God for rebelling against David. He adds that the men died in the forest when they became entangled in the forest growth. See the next note.

64. The popular thought, mentioned in the Babylonian Talmud *Sotah* 9b, that Absalom's long hair got caught in a limb is not supported by the text which states that his head was caught in the tree.

realized he had acted improperly and wanted to atone. He hoped that if he allowed David's men to kill him, this would expiate his wrong not go to Hell.[65]

A soldier saw Absalom hanging from the tree and reported it to his commander Joab, who shouted that the soldier should have killed him. The soldier said that no money in the world would prompt him to kill David's son for he heard David say that they should treat Absalom well. Joab responded by shooting Absalom with three darts. Ten of his men then jumped upon Absalom and killed him.

Joab blew his horn signaling that the battle should stop. Absalom's men fled home. Joab buried Absalom. Scripture states that Absalom had erected a pillar as a monument to his life, where he would be buried and remembered, but instead, Joab buried him in a pit and covered him with stones.[66]

WHY DID JOAB KILL ABSALOM?

Throughout their long relationship, Joab continually acted to protect his cousin David and to help him in any way that he could. Unfortunately, being human, Joab did not always do what David wanted done. An example is his killing of Abner.[67] Granted he slew Abner in revenge for Abner murdering his brother. Granted also that he may have feared that Abner would succeed in obtaining the command of David's army. But he also did it to assure that Saul's son Ish-bosheth would have no military leadership to oppose David and stop him from becoming king of the united tribes. Yet, despite his good intention to aid him, David did not like what he did, for it caused the northern tribes to rile against him.

Similarly, here. Although II Samuel does not give Joab's reason for killing Absalom, we can assume that he thought that as long as Absalom lived, even if he were imprisoned, a segment of the people would seek to free him, follow him, and make him king.

---

65. Maimonides wrote in his essay called Chelek that a person who accepts what a Midrash states as being the truth is a fool. One who feels that since Midrashic tales are untrue, one should ignore them, is also a fool, because the untrue Midrashim were composed as parables to teach lessons. It may be that while the story of Absalom's meditation is false and there is no Hell, the rabbis are teaching that one should correct behavior as soon as possible.
66. Josephus (*Antiquities* 7, 10, 3) states that in his time, around 100 CE, the site of the monument was unknown.
67. Chapter 3.

NOTIFICATION GIVEN TO DAVID OF HIS SON'S DEATH

Ahimaaz was the son of one of the two senior priests whom David had requested to go to Jerusalem with the ark and notify him of all significant events occurring there. He was one of those two sons who gave David information about Absalom's planned attack.[68] He volunteered to Joab to tell David about the victory. Worried about David's reaction upon hearing that Absalom had been killed,[69] Joab did not allow Ahimaaz to go but sent a Cushite.[70] Ahimaaz begged Joab to allow him to run after the Cushite and support the news that the latter gave David, and Joab allowed him to do so. But Ahimaaz ran faster than the Cushite and reached David first.

When David asked Ahimaaz for news of his son, Ahimaaz answered that he did not know. Then the Cushite arrived and told the king the bad news, he had won the war, but his son was dead.

WHY IS THIS EPISODE ABOUT AHIMAAZ INSERTED HERE?

It highlights the despair that affected David since his bedding of Bat-sheba, the tragedies that filled his life from that time until his death. David's forces were successful in defeating Absalom's army. Ahimaaz who knew this and knew that Absalom was dead wanted to give what he considered good news to David whom he had helped just before the battle began.[71] Yet, when Ahimaaz saw the anguish in David's face, he was unable to give what he now realized was bad news to the man he loved.

---

68. Verses 15:36, 17:15ff.
69. David had killed the man who told him about Saul and Jonathan's death.
70. Probably an Ethiopian slave whom Joab felt would not be as great a loss as Ahimaaz. Radak, ever worried that David should have no non-Israelite in his army, asserts that the man was an Israelite, a man from Cush who converted, or an Israelite with such dark skin that people called him a Cushite.
71. 17:15–22.

David exacerbates the animosity of the northern tribes

II SAMUEL 19

Two events follow the war: (1) David's great grief and (2) his failure to quiet the discontent of the non-Judean tribes, and his aggravation over it.

DAVID IGNORES HIS PEOPLE WHILE HE GRIEVES

David's mourning over Absalom's death was excessive. He secluded himself, "and he said as he went: 'My son Absalom, my son, my son Absalom! If only I had died instead of you! Absalom, my son, my son!'" He mentioned his son's name three times in this short lament and the word "son" five times.

When Joab heard that David had turned the victory into a time of mourning and that the people were disappointed, he advised David that unless he stop his exaggerated mourning, his people would abandon him. David listened to him, left his seclusion, sat by the gate, and all the people came to see him.

While Joab led David's forces to victory, David relieved him of his command because he killed Absalom, and appointed another of his relatives to lead his army.

DAVID'S GRIEF

Why, after not seeking Absalom for three years when his son was in self-imposed exile with his grandfather and then two years when Absalom returned to Israel, and only spoke to him when persuaded to do so by the wise woman of Tekoa, did David grieve with such intensity when he heard that Absalom was dead? Many parents love their child who makes a very bad mistake, but feel that the child needs some kind of punishment, and it is possible that this was in David's mind.[72]

---

72. Dr. Norman Wald, my study partner suggested this idea.

DAVID AGGRAVATES THE DISCONTENT OF THE
NORTHERN TRIBES AGAINST JUDAH

Verses 9 and 10 state "Israel [the defeated non-Judean tribes] fled every man to his tent. And all the people were at strife throughout all the tribes of Israel." They were conflicted. They recalled how David "saved us out of the hand of the Philistines," yet they abandoned him, and "Absalom, whom we appointed over us, is dead in battle," and the ancient grievances against Judah remained. Nevertheless, they felt that they should return and show loyalty to David by joining in the procession "of bringing the king back [to Jerusalem]."[73] But although they were well meaning and this presented an opportunity for reconciliation, David ignored them. He requested that the Judeans, members of his tribe, lead his return.

David further aggravated the northern tribes by how he treated Mephibosheth, Saul's grandson, who came to greet the king. Mephibosheth mourned for David during the entire time of David's retreat by not washing his feet or his clothes or trimming his beard. He explained that Ziba had deceived him when he told him he did not need to come to David because he promised to tell David that it was difficult for him to come because he was lame. He insisted that Ziba lied to David when he reported that Mephibosheth was planning to become king of Israel. Instead of listening to Mephibosheth's justification of his behavior, David cut him off in the middle of his explanation and decided on a compromise; Ziba would not keep all of King Saul's property, as he previously promised, but only half.

David failed to realize that this compromise signaled to the non-Judean supporters of Mephibosheth that David was unsure of Mephibosheth's loyalty. Intended or not, this act of apparent uncertainty about allegiances was a snub not only to Mephibosheth but also to all of the non-Judean tribes. As a result, "all the people of Judah brought the king over, and also [only] half the people of Israel."[74]

Shimei, who had cursed David during his retreat and cast stones at him, came to greet David with a thousand men, and asked David to forgive him for his prior acts. David swore to Shimei that he would not die.[75] Ziba, Mephibosheth's servant,

---

73. Verses 10 and 11.
74. Verse 41.
75. Yet, on his death bed, In 1 Kings 2, when he no longer feared Shimei's influence with the northern tribes, he told his son and heir Solomon to kill Shimei.

also came to greet the king with his fifteen sons and twenty servants.[76] So too Barzillai, who brought David and his troop food, came.[77]

The men of Israel came to David and asked why he favored Judah over them by having Judah lead the return. David again missed an opportunity and did not answer, letting his insensitive Judean leaders respond. "And all the men of Judah answered the men of Israel: 'Because the king is a near of kin to us; why are you angry about the matter.... ' And the men of Israel answered the men of Judah, and said: 'We have ten parts in the king [since we are ten tribes], and we have also more right in David than you; why then did you despise us.... ' And the words of the men of Judah were fiercer than the words of the men of Israel."[78]

Thus it is no surprise that in the next chapter, Israel rebelled again against David. David won this new rebellion as he did his war with Absalom. But when the people rose up once more under the leadership of Jeroboam of the northern tribes against his grandson Rehoboam, Rehoboam was no David, and the kingdom was split.

THE TALMUD'S APPARENT SUPPORT OF THIS INTERPRETATION

The Babylonian Talmud, *Shabbat* 56a and b, discusses whether Kings David and Solomon acted properly. In 56b, the Talmud focuses on II Samuel 19 and reports a view that David treated Saul's grandson Mephibosheth improperly:

> Rab Judah said in Rab's name: "When David said to Mephibosheth, 'Thou and Ziba divide the land,' a Heavenly Echo came forth and declared to him, 'Rehoboam and Jeroboam shall divide the kingdom.' " Rab Judah said in Rab's name: "Had not David paid heed to slander, the kingdom of the House of David would not have been divided, Israel not engaged in idolatry [when Jeroboam set up golden calves for worship], and we would not have been exiled from our country."[79]

At first blush, this punishment of the division of the kingdom that affected not only David but all Judeans and Israelites until today – leading to idol worship and exile – seems to be an excessive response for an action as simple as dividing King

---

76. No information is given as to what they said or did.
77. Mentioned in 17:27ff. David requests Solomon to care for Barzillai's sons in I Kings 2:7.
78. Verses 43–44.
79. Babylonian Talmud, *Seder Mo'ed*, 56b.

Saul's property between Saul's grandson and Ziba, who was a servant of King Saul. However, once it is understood that the Talmud is focusing on David's failure to consider the needs and feelings of the non-Judean tribes, we understand that the Talmud is correct. The Talmud's statement is a parable written to capture this point: the split in the Davidic kingdom and all that followed was the natural consequence of David's misguided behavior, just as there were natural consequences from his affair with Bat-sheba.

David should have remembered that the non-Judean tribes saw Mephibosheth, Saul's grandson, as having the right to serve as king. They had, in fact, joined Absalom against Judah because they were dissatisfied with David's rule. They probably felt that once Absalom beat David and wrested the kingdom from him, they could take it from Absalom and give it to Mephibosheth, one of their own. This was the gist of Ziba's "slander" against Mephibosheth.

This was a terrible mistake by David. He should have predicted that the non-Judean tribes would take his behavior to Mephibosheth as an insult to him and to all non-Judeans. Thus, as the Talmud relates, David's behavior was another in a string of inappropriate and insensitive behaviors that the non-Judeans considered – along with Rehoboam's insult – the straw that broke the camel's back. The weakness of the divided kingdom ultimately led to defeat by the Assyrians and Babylonians and exile. David's mistake had terrible natural consequences.

Joab Retakes Command

II SAMUEL 20

David, as described in the prior chapter, not only failed to appease the northern tribes who seem to have joined his son Absalom in his rebellion against David, but he aggravated their long-standing displeasure of the tribe of Judah, and the anger of some members of the norther tribes escalated into another rebellion.

SHEBA'S REBELLION

Sheba was a Benjamite, as was King Saul. He was present when only the tribe of Judah led David back to Jerusalem. He summoned the northerners together with a blast of a shofar and shouted, "'We have no portion in David . . . every man to his tents Israel.' So every man from Israel [the northern tribes] left David and followed Sheba."[80]

Sheba's revolt could cause more trouble than Absalom. Absalom's revolt threatened the king; Sheba's threatened the kingdom itself. It showed that the allegiance of the northern tribes to the house of David had become tenuous.

Before responding to the revolt, David felt he had to demonstrate that he was in control. Absalom had made his bedding of David's concubines his first act showing his control of the kingdom. He no longer wanted to bed these women. His first act in Jerusalem was to place them in a guarded house and provide for their needs. He then summoned Amasa, the former commander of Absalom's army, whom he had placed as his commander instead of Joab, and ordered him to call the men of Judah together within three days.

We have no idea about Amasa's loyalty or why David chose him as his commander other than he wanted to reduce Joab's role in his army, because, as usual,

---

80. Verses 1 and 2. The words "all of Israel" is hyperbole

the Bible is silent on what people think. But we are told here that Amasa was unable to gather the Judeans within the three-day period. Was this former Absalom commander sympathetic to the claims of the north? Did David make a mistake in appointing him his general? Was Amasa's inability to gather the Judeans due to his inability, his lack of vigor? Did he fail because the Judeans did not want to be led by the former Absalom commander? Should we understand that David appointed Amasa as supreme commander as a diplomatic tactic, as a Republican president may put a Democrat into his cabinet with the hope that it will help unite the country, but in the case of Amasa the tactic did not work? Is this incident a sign that David is no longer thinking well? We do not know.

David turned to Abishai, his cousin, Joab's brother, still neglecting Joab, and commanded him to pursue Sheba immediately, hoping to capture him before he is able to lodge in a fortified city. Abishai did not capture Sheba before he fortified himself. He was no Joab. But he could summon the army. Joab's men, the mercenaries Cherethites and Pelethites, "and all the mighty men" joined in the pursuit of Sheba.[81]

During the march north, Amasa joined Abishai with the troops he could muster. Joab, not Abishai, went out to great him. His sword fell from his scabbard and he picked it up and held it in his left hand. Amasa did not feel threatened. Joab embraced Amasa with his right hand, and stabbed him with his left.[82]

One of Joab's men then called to the forces that Amasa mustered and said, "He who favors Joab, and he who is for David, follow Joab." And "all the people followed Joab to pursue Sheba."[83] Significantly, while David had replaced Joab with Amasa and then Abishai, the army followed Joab. This explains why despite David being displeased with many of Joab's acts, he was unable to kill him, and it was only on his death bed that he instructed his son Solomon to do so.[84]

---

81. Verse 7.

82. The details of the event are obscure. It is likely that Joab planned to surprise Amasa. He let his sword fall while adjusting his scabbard and picked it up with his left hand so that Amasa would not feel threatened. It is also obscure why Joab killed Amasa. We can recall his murder of Abner who he may have thought at the time would assume his position as head of David's army. He may have killed Amasa for the same reason or he murdered him out of his love for David, for he may have felt that the former head of Absalom's army was not trustworthy and David was making a mistake in trusting him.

83. Verses 11 and 13.

84. I Kings 2.

SHEBA'S DEATH

Sheba fled to a fortified city, and Joab besieged it. A "wise woman" called out to Joab requesting that he come near so that she could speak to him.[85] She said to Joab, "There is an ancient saying: 'You must ask at Abel. And this ended the matter.'"[86]

THE MEANING OF THE WISE WOMAN'S PROVERB

The simple meaning of the words seems to be: Instead of besieging our town Abel, you should have come first and spoken with us and we could have settled the matter to everyone's satisfaction (that is, everyone other than Sheba). But most commentators read the words as having another meaning. Many ideas have been offered to explain the cryptic proverb about Abel and whether the woman lived in Abel the city that was besieged, or Abel was a neighboring town.

Hertzberg states that the meaning of the proverb is no longer recoverable from the text. It may refer to the neighboring city of Abel that "made a particularly large contribution to the settling of disputes and the relaxing of disputes in Israel."[87] Goldman suggests that Abel was the surrounded city. Driver supposes that Abel was well-known for having wise inhabitants, and the proverb arose saying these people should be consulted before undertaking a difficult endeavor. The Targum, followed by Rashi, Radak, and Altschuler, understands that the wise woman is referring to Deuteronomy 20:10ff where the Bible stresses that a besieging army should first ask a besieged city to surrender: "You should have first asked that the city of Abel surrender peacefully." *Midrash Tanchuma* elaborates upon this notion, and where verse 17 has the wise woman asking "Are you Joab," understands her saying are you the same Joab who we are told studies Torah? How come you forgot the law of Deuteronomy 20:10ff?"

The wise woman continued after her initial words and said: "We are a peaceful city, why destroy us?" Joab answered that he was seeking the rebel Sheba. "Hand

---

85. *Midrash Shemuel* 32:3 identifies the wise woman as the granddaughter of the patriarch Jacob, Serah the daughter of Asher, who, according to a tradition was the person who informed Jacob that his son Joseph was still alive. Jacob was so overjoyed that he blessed her that she should live an extremely long life. Abarbanel comments that if she is the wise woman, she would be, according to his calculation, 684 years old during the days of David.

86. Verse 18.

87. Page 373.

him to me and we will depart." She replied that the inhabitants would throw She-ba's head over the wall to Joab.[88] The people of the city agreed with the woman and did what she suggested. And Joab "blew the horn, and they left the city, every man to his tent. And Joab returned to Jerusalem to the king."[89]

THE TWO WISE WOMEN

The discussion of the wise woman and Joab here should remind readers of the audience of the wise woman from Tekoa in chapter 14 with David. The wise woman of Tekoa advised David to set aside the interest of society (the law as understood at that time) in favor of the interests of one man, Absalom, which resulted in a rebellion. In contrast, this wise woman counseled Joab to sacrifice one man, Sheba, in the interest of society as a whole, resulting in the prevention of a rebellion (McCarter).

DAVID'S OFFICIALS

Chapter 20 ends with a list of David's officials. They are essentially the same as in 8:16ff. There are two significant differences: David's sons are no longer mentioned as priests. No reason is given for their removal from the position. Goldman suggests that it may have been prompted by Absalom's rebellion. He may be suggesting that David feared future rebellions from his sons and felt that it was best not to give them too much power. The tactic did not work, as seen in the rebellion of another son in 1 Kings 1.

The second difference is that David now appointed Adoram as head of labor gangs, a system of forced labor. This was a terrible mistake with terrible conse-quences. It appears that this system of corvée first began at the end of David's reign. It was later expanded during the reign of his son Solomon who engaged in huge building endeavors, including the building of his palace and the first temple.

---

88. She may have refrained from opening the gate and giving Sheba to Joab out of prudent fear. Joab was known to kill precipitously. He had killed Absalom against David's order as well as others, and just murdered Amasa. She may have feared that Joab would consider the city guilty of harboring Sheba until the city was surrounded.

89. Verse 22. Rashi reads this verse to imply that Joab was reinstated as chief commander of David's army.

The people disliked the forced labor and taxes that Solomon imposed upon them to pay for the buildings, and stoned Adoram, rebelled against Solomon's son Rehoboam, and established a new kingdom in the north.[90]

90. I Kings 12:18.

PART 6
Appendices

As with many other biblical books, the book of Samuel ends with added material that does not follow the preceding chapters. We do not know when the deeds mentioned in chapters 21–24 occurred, but it is certain that they did not happen at the end of David's life. It is possible that the editor had this material and did not know where to place it. It is also possible that after the book was finished with chapter 20, another man or men decided to add the other traditions, but did not want to meddle with what was already written.

This phenomenon is not unique. It occurs also, for example, at the end of the books of Joshua and Judges and in Ecclesiastes as well. Also the ending of the book of Ruth, which speaks about Ruth's descendant being David, about which neither Samuel nor Kings notices, is most likely a late addition.

Chapter 20 is not the end of the story of King David. The end is in 1 Kings 1 and 2, which tell of David's death and serve as an introduction to the tale of Solomon's reign.

Why Did God Kill Saul's Children for Saul's Improper Act?

II SAMUEL 21

II Samuel 21 relates a remarkable tale that troubled the talmudic rabbis. The rabbis' solution does not address all of the problems raised by this chapter and may not satisfy modern sensibilities of justice.

THE FOLLOWING TRANSPIRED IN THIS CHAPTER:

1. In the time of King David's rule, there was a famine for three years.
2. King David asked why God sent the famine.
3. God replied, "It is for Saul and his bloody house because he put to death the Gibeonites [non-Israelites]" (II Samuel 21:1). Saul had slain the Gibeonites "in his zeal for the children of Israel and Judah" (II Samuel 21:2). The chapter does not state when or why Saul killed Gibeonites.
4. David asked the Gibeonites how he could atone for Saul's misdeed.
5. The Gibeonites replied, "Let seven men of his [Saul's] sons be delivered unto us, and we will hang them up unto the Lord" (II Samuel 21:6).
6. David said, "I will deliver them" (II Samuel 21:6). He did, but did not include Jonathan's son Mephibosheth.
7. The Gibeonites killed them and hanged their dead bodies "in the mountain before the Lord" (II Samuel 21:9).

QUESTIONS

1. When did this episode occur?
2. Why did David ask God what the reason was for the famine instead of asking how the famine could be stopped?

3. What right did God have to punish all of the innocent Israelites with a three-year famine for the misdeed of a single individual, Saul? Deuteronomy 24:16 commands, "Neither shall the children be put to death for the fathers."

4. Why did David seek atonement from the Gibeonites and not from God?

5. What right did David have to allow seven innocent sons of Saul to be killed for the misbehavior of their father?

6. What is the talmudic explanation of this chapter?

7. What is a reasonable explanation of the chapter based on the Maimonidean method?

THE TALMUDIC EXPLANATION OF CHAPTER 21

The Babylonian Talmud, *Yevamot* 78b and 79a, states that David used the Urim and Thummim, an object mentioned in the Torah and employed to communicate with God, to find out why a famine struck the land.[1] He found out that the famine resulted from Saul's improper act of killing the Gibeonites and because Saul was not "mourned in a proper manner." The second reason was apparently given to explain why the innocent Israelites, who should have mourned their king, were killed in the famine.[2]

This talmudic source minimizes the impropriety of Saul's unlawful killing of the Gibeonites somewhat by saying that Saul only killed them indirectly. He "killed the inhabitants of Nob, the city of the priests who were supplying them [the Gibeonites] with water and food. Scripture regards it as if he himself had killed them."[3]

David, the Talmud continues, "tried to pacify them [the Gibeonites] but they would not be pacified." When the Gibeonites demanded the sons of Saul, "They

---

1. The Bible does not explain exactly what the Urim and Thummim was, how it functioned, or how long the Israelites used it. It is not mentioned after the Five Books of Moses other than once where it states that Saul did not use it (1 Samuel 28:6). It is possible that the authors of the later books knew nothing about it and the Saul reference was a later addition. The Talmud states that it was used in this episode, but the Bible itself does not say so.

2. The *Midrash Pirkei d'Rabbi Eliezer* states that the famine was brought because David failed to bury Saul. Abarbanel writes that the Israelites were killed for not stopping Saul from killing the Gibeonites.

3. The quote is from the Soncino translation of The Babylonian Talmud.

were made to pass before the Holy Ark. He whom the Ark retained[4] [was condemned] to death and he whom the Ark did not retain was saved alive."

The Jerusalem Talmud *Kiddushin* 65c speculates that Saul killed seven Gibeonites. The Babylonian Talmud *Yevamot* 78b supposes that Gibeonites worked for the priests at Nob. Saul had all the priests at Nob killed (1 Samuel 22:18) and the Gibeonites had no work, and this was equivalent to killing them. None of this is stated in Samuel.

What was the guilt of the sons? Two answers are offered by the Babylonian Talmud: (1) They were involved with their father in the killing of the Gibeonites. (2) "It is better that a letter be rooted out of the Torah than that the divine name shall be publicly profaned." The latter statement means that it is proper to overlook a biblical command when the result of obeying it would be profaning God. In this case, a profanation would have occurred if the crime against the Gibeonites had been allowed to go unpunished.

Similarly, the Talmud recognizes that Saul's sons were left hanging for months in violation of Deuteronomy 21:23, "His body shall not remain all night on the tree," but explains, "It is proper that a letter be rooted out of the Torah so that thereby the heavenly name shall be hallowed." For passersby would see them hanging and would ask, "What kind of men are these?" When told that they were Israelite princes who were punished for killing non-Israelites, passersby would be impressed, for the Torah is as concerned about non-Israelites as it is about Israelites. In fact, the Talmud states that as a result of the hanging, "A hundred and fifty thousand men immediately joined Israel."[5]

WHEN DID THE EVENTS OCCUR?

There are essentially two approaches to the understanding of chapter 21. The talmudic passages above takes the biblical text literally and adds imaginative details. *Talmud!* The second respects the Bible as much as the first, but states that Scripture should be mined to determine what it is really saying. The second approach also recognizes that biblical personalities can do wrong. In reading this chapter, it suggests that King David performed acts that the average Jew would find objectionable, and therefore Scripture only hinted at it, but did not state it explicitly.

---

4. Apparently those who were held fast and not allowed to leave.

5. A similar answer is given in *Numbers Rabba* 5.

Our analysis begins with deciding when this episode occurred. Knowing when David acted can help us understand why he did what he did.

Although chapters 21 to 24 are placed at the conclusion of II Samuel, the general consensus among scholars, as previously stated, is that the events did not take place at the end of David's forty-year reign, but at different times during his earlier life. The prevailing view is that the events occurred after the death of King Saul, after David had served as king of Judah for seven years and six months. He had just become king over the united twelve tribes and was looking for ways to secure his reign.

WHY DID DAVID ASK GOD WHY GOD SENT THE FAMINE?

We should note that while the Bible states that David asked God why he sent the famine, it does not mention that David asked God what to do about it, which is the more important question. It is reasonable to understand that the Bible does not intend that its readers take the incident literally. David may have asked this question of himself, not God. Thus, we need to revise the question to: what prompted David to consider the famine at this time? Why was it only after three years that David began to deal with this problem? The answer to this question only becomes evident after asking and answering other questions.

What right did God have in punishing the innocent Israelites for Saul's misdeed? Additionally, if the famine was a punishment, why was a famine chosen and not something else?

It is obvious that a merciful and just God does not punish innocent people for a guilty person's act. However, a guilty person's behavior can create a series of consequences that affect innocent parties. We saw this phenomenon of cause and effect in many chapters following David's behavior with Bat-sheba. This is natural and is not the miraculous intervention of God into human affairs. As Maimonides explains in his *Guide of the Perplexed* 2:48, the Bible very frequently ascribes a natural occurrence to God to inform its readers that, although the event was an expected result of the laws of nature and God did not interfere with nature to produce it, God created the laws of nature.

This Maimonidean understanding of Scripture answers our questions. God was not directly involved in the episode. It is reasonable to understand that the famine was the natural result of the devastating wars that Saul was engaged in, wars that ruined the produce of the land. It is easy to realize that the two contesting forces destroyed the harvest to stop their enemies from living off of the land. But by doing so, they ruined their own ability to eat after the cessation of hostilities. There are numerous examples of these deeds in history. This is what the Bible means when it states that the famine was the result of Saul's bloody deeds with the Gibeonites.

WHY DID DAVID SEEK A RESOLUTION OF THE PROBLEM FROM THE GIBEONITES?

David wanted to use the devastating situation to his best political advantage. He had just assumed the reign over the united twelve tribes. Saul was dead, but some of his sons were still alive. Looking at the chapter from a historical and political perspective, we recognize that David knew that if a situation arose in which he showed weakness, the northern tribes, who disliked his tribe Judah, would usurp the kingdom from him and hand it to Saul's sons. This is exactly what they attempted to do during the rebellion by Sheba.

David's only solution, a solution followed by virtually all ancient kings, was to remove the threat by killing Saul's sons. But how could he do so without provoking the anger and rebellion of the northern tribes who were loyal to Saul's family? He realized that he could have them killed by exploiting the famine and blaming Saul's sons' deaths on the non-Israelite Gibeonites.[6]

---

6. Several other adventures are narrated in this chapter. (1) Prompted by one of King Saul's concubines, David rescued the bodies of Saul and his son Jonathan from the men of Jabesh-gilead who had stolen them from the Philistines (1 Samuel 31:12f) and had them buried in the sepulcher of Saul's father Kish. (2) During a battle against Philistines, which was led by David, David became faint and a giant nearly killed him, but he was rescued by Abishai, his cousin, who killed the giant. (3) In another war against Philistines, Elhanan slew the giant Goliath the Gittite. See my book *Who Really Was the Biblical David?*, 1 Samuel 16 and 17, which discusses whether this conflicts with chapter 17 which states that David killed Goliath.

David's Words of Thanks

II SAMUEL 22 – 23

The fifty-one verses in chapter 22 contain David's song of triumph composed, according to verse 1, "in the day that the Lord saved him from the hand of every enemy and the hand of Saul."

Seven of the verses in chapter 23 are called in verse 1, "the final words of David." David's testament, his real last words, are in 1 Kings 2:2ff.

PROBLEM WITH CHAPTER 22

This hymn, although placed at the end of Samuel, like chapter 21, describes an event, even as the verse states, when David was saved from Saul's attempts to kill him. The hymn was also placed in the book of Psalms as Psalm 18. There are differences in the wording of the two versions. Some of the differences are due to scribal errors. Scholars think the other differences are due to the Samuel version being the original one and Psalm 18 "having been subjected to a literary revision at a later date" (Goldman). Why the writer of Psalm 18 felt he had the right to change David's words, especially since a reader of Samuel would see the change and Jewish tradition considers both books sacred parts of the Bible, is inexplicable, unless we say that the author of Psalms did not consider Samuel sacred. Or, perhaps, we should redefine the word sacred. It does not mean that God dictated the words. It means that the text is important because it teaches us the history of the Jews and contains many lessons, but it is a human inspired document.[7]

---

7. The identical problem exists in respect to the biblical book of Chronicles. It adds to and detracts from the books of Samuel and Kings, offers different events, attributes events to people other than what is mentioned in the prior books, and frequently spells names differently.

FINAL THIRTY-TWO VERSES OF CHAPTER 23

In the introductory seven verses of chapter 23, David asserts "The spirit of the Lord (*ruach y-h-v-h*) spoke by me, and his words are on my tongue," apparently claiming that God was speaking though him, but the words could be understood to mean that what follows are his own thoughts, but he feels close to God and inspired. He goes on to say that God called him righteous: "The righteous shall rule over men, he who rules with the fear of God." He states that God "made an everlasting covenant with me," which some commentators see as a referral to the prophets promise in 7:12, that after David's death, God "will set up your seed after you, which come from your body, and I will establish his kingdom," which could refer to Solomon succeeding him, or to a long line of David's descendants ruling after him,[8] or to the messiah.[9] *The misskh!*

Verses 8–39 list David's men, or some of them, and tell very briefly how the men distinguished themselves. The list is repeated in 1 Chronicles 11–41 with many differences in spelling and in what the men accomplished. The list is noteworthy in not including Joab as David's supreme commander and in the repeated use of the number three. For example, Josheb-basshebeth was a chief of the three, as was Adino who in Samuel is said to have killed eight hundred enemy soldiers, but the number is three hundred in Chronicles. Dodo was one of the three mighty men who were with David. Similarly, verse 13 describes an exploit by "three of the thirty chiefs" who broke though Philistine lines to bring David water. And there are close to a dozen other mentions of three. There are mistakes in the list: verse 24 states that Asahel was one of the thirty, but thirty-one names are listed, and Chronicles 11 has sixteen more. All told, verse 39 states there were "thirty-seven in all," but only thirty-six are listed.

---

8. This is a hyperbolic statement which should not be understood that every ruler of the united-kingdom of Judah and Israel will be David's descendants.

9. See Goldman and others on 7:12.

Did David Do Wrong When
He Counted People?

II SAMUEL 24

The final chapter of II Samuel, chapter 24, contains one of the most incomprehensible stories in the Bible, an inexplicable theological event. Verse 1 reports that "the anger of the Lord was continued against Israel, and he [God] incited David against them [Israel], saying, 'Go, number Israel and Judah.'" David succumbed to the incitement and instructed his supreme commander Joab to assemble soldiers to tally the people. After counting for nine months and twenty days, Joab returned to the capital and reported that he counted eight hundred thousand Israelite males who could be mobilized for war as well as five hundred thousand men with similar martial qualifications from the tribe of Judah.[10]

QUESTIONS

1. Why was God's anger "*continued* against Israel"? "Continued" after what?
2. Does the all-wise deity succumb to anger?
3. Does God become involved in human affairs to the extent that "He incited David" to act improperly?
4. Does God's incitement of David reveal that at least sometimes people do not have free will?
5. Why should people be punished for their actions if God forces them to act in a certain way?
6. What was the purpose of the census?

---

10. I Chronicles 21:5 gives the number for Israel as 1,100,000 and for Judah 470,000.

7. Why did David send his general and his soldiers and not civil servants to perform the census?

8. Why did David later call the census a "great" mistake?

9. Why wasn't David's repentance, which occurred before anyone else commented on his act, accepted by God and stopped God from punishing David's people?

10. Why were seventy thousand innocent people punished with death as a result of David's improper act?

11. What is the connection between the census and the plague killing so many people?

12. What is the significance of the placement of an altar on the threshing-floor of Araunah the Jebusite?

13. Why was the tribe of Judah counted separately from the other tribes?

14. What is the meaning of "David's heart smote him"?

SOME EXPLANATIONS BY TRADITIONAL BIBLE COMMENTATORS

Rashi and Radak state they do not know why God is angry here. Rabbi Zev Bar Eitan describes Abarbanel's view that counting people provokes an evil eye and God wanted to punish many Israelites for failing to accept David as their king and joining in Sheba's rebellion.[11] "This count brought ignominy in the form of the evil eye. The resulting plague reached mammoth proportions. Unwittingly, King David had been Heaven's accomplice to right the wrongs of a nation hell-bent on ousting their righteous monarch.... (W)ithout divine intervention, the destructive capability of the unchecked evil eye mows down indiscriminately."

Eitan also mentions that King Saul recognized the danger of the evil eye when he counted the nation in 1 Samuel 11:8 and 15:4. To avoid the evil eye, Saul performed the count in the first instance by "utilizing a goat collection and on the second occasion he demanded smooth little pebbles." While, this is Abarbanel's interpretation of Saul's two censuses, the text does not say that Saul feared an evil eye, not does it say that he made the count by using goats or pebbles. The Babylonian Talmud *Yoma* 22b does say that Saul made the count using goats but not in regard to 11:8, as Abarbanel states, but 15:4.

What is the evil eye? Nobody really knows because it is simply a superstitious

---

11. Zev Bar-Eitan, *Abravanel's World of Torah* (Renaissance Torah Press, 2016), 160 and 161. The spelling of Abarbanel's name (1437–1508) varies. Bar-Eitan prefers the spelling he uses.

belief, it does not exist, and those who believe it exists are afraid to investigate it lest their investigation prompt the evil eye to harm them. It is likely that the evil eye is the belief that doing certain acts can be seen by some demons who punish the perpetrator for the act.

ArtScroll states that although the text does not say what angered God, it is a basic principle that God is provoked to anger when people act improperly. Maimonides rejects the view that God can become angry and explains that the Torah states that God is angry to frighten people not to do wrong.[12]

Nachmanides asserts that God was angry because the people did not join David in his request to build a temple. According to Nachmanides, God wanted a temple and would have told David to build it if the people expressed a desire to have it.[13] I Chronicles 21:1 and the Aramaic Targum to II Samuel 24 state that Satan enticed David.

Nachmanides explains that the Torah only allows an indirect count, such as having each man donate a shekel and counting the shekels.[14]

The Babylonian Talmud *Berakhot* 62b states that David is being punished for saying to Saul in I Samuel 26:19 that he bears the king no grudge, but it is Saul's fault that there is enmity between them, "God incited you against me." The Talmud imagines God saying angrily, "You accused me of being an inciter. I swear, I will incite you to do something that even school children know is not allowed [to make a head count of people]."

Gersonides supposes that David counted people because he relied on the human power of his army and not God.

Virtually all of these suggestions, attempts to explain an obscure text, rely on superstitious ideas, and belittle God by reading the text literally and thinking that God can be overcome by anger to the extent of killing people who caused the anger.

•

DAVID REGRETS HIS ACT

As David listens to the report of the many deaths, he thinks back on what he did and is sorry he undertook the census project. Verse 10 reveals that, "David's

---

12. *Guide of the Perplexed* 1:55 and many other chapters where Maimonides states that God has no emotions.

13. Nachmanides to Numbers 16:21.

14. Commentaries to Exodus 30:12 and Numbers 1:3.

heart smote him after he had numbered the people. And David said to the Lord, 'I acted badly by doing what I did. Now Lord, erase the misdeed of your servant, for I have been very foolish.'"

After David recognizes the foolish nature of his act and repents, the prophet Gad appears to him. Gad says that God will allow David to choose between three punishments: "Should seven years of famine come to your land? Or would you flee for three months from your foes while they pursue you? Or should there be three days of plague in your land?"[15]

In verse 14, faced with these three grave options, David decides, seemingly wisely, to leave the decision to the all-knowing merciful deity. "David said to Gad: 'I am in great straits. Let us now fall into the hand of the Lord, for his mercies are great, and let me not fall into the hand of man.'" David's strategy does not work.[16]

Verse 15 reveals that God selects the third option and kills seventy thousand of David's people. "So the Lord sent a plague upon Israel from the morning until the appointed time. And there died of the people from Dan even to Beer Sheba seventy thousand men." The plague stops at the threshing-floor of Araunah the Jebusite in Jerusalem.

Upon seeing that many of his people died in the plague, David "spoke to the Lord when he saw the angel that smote the people, and said: 'True, I did wrong and acted improperly. But these sheep [people], what have they done? Let your hand please be against me, and my father's house and not against them.'"

The text states "God relented of the evil and told the angel who was destroying the people, 'Enough, stay your hand!'"[17]

Gad returns God's answer, "Go up and set an altar for God on the threshing-floor of Araunah the Jebusite."[18]

Maimonides would reject any desire to read this verse literally. He was convinced that God makes no mistakes from which a change is necessary. He also interpreted the word "angel" to mean any part of nature that accomplishes God's

---

15. Verse 13.

16. This could be interpreted as follows: God is not involved. David realizes that there could be three consequences. He is frozen in doubt, passive, unable to decide what to do. So nature takes its course.

17. Verse 16.

18. Verse 17f.

will. We should interpret the verse simply that the plague ran its course and stopped.

What does the setting of the ark on the threshing-floor have to do with this episode? It is reasonable to suppose that David saw that the plague had stopped, and by his own initiative or by the advice of Gad, he arranged for a public thank-you to God, a demonstration that would please the people. It also served as a memorial to remind David not to act again as he had acted; he must consider the consequences of his behavior. This is especially important for a leader whose actions so directly affect the lives of his people.

WHAT PRIOR ACT BY THE ISRAELITES INCITED THE CONTINUANCE OF GOD'S ANGER?

In an essay in *Tanakh Companion to the Book of Samuel*, Rabbi David Silber suggests that God was still angry that Saul had massacred the Gibeonites after Joshua and the Israelites had taken an oath not to harm them. Scripture does not mention this war.

Once again, referring to Maimonides' understanding of God's involvement in the world can help readers understand what appears to be a miraculous and perplexing occurrence in a more rational and natural manner. We can build on Rabbi Silber's interpretation by referring to the insight of Maimonides in his *Guide of the Perplexed* 2:48. Maimonides teaches that when the Bible states that God does something, it means that the recorded event occurred according to the laws of nature, reminding the reader that God created the laws of nature and is, therefore, indirectly responsible for what occurs.

Understanding the text in this way, we can posit that the Bible is certainly not implying that God can become angry and retain a fit of anger for generations. Instead, the Bible is informing the reader that certain unforeseen natural events occurred as a result of Saul's war with the Gibeonites. Saul failed to consider all possible results of his massacre. He may have left the mass of decomposing bodies unburied, resulting in a plague that affected the growth of produce. It is also possible that the famine was the result of the burning of fields during the battle so that the enemy soldiers would have no food. The Bible does not reveal any details.

Thus, when the Bible says that God *continued* to be angry, we can understand that it is stating that David was about to make the same mistake as Saul, not taking time to consider the consequences of his behavior and, as with Saul, unforeseen natural results followed.

DID GOD FORCE DAVID TO DO WHAT HE DID?

Following the insight of *Guide of the Perplexed* 2:48, we can now speculate that the Bible's intent is that David made the decision himself, without divine involvement, using his reasoning ability, according to the laws of nature created by God.[19]

David was involved in warfare virtually his entire life. It is reasonable to assume that he undertook the census to see how many men he could muster for an anticipated battle.

That the census was to procure potential soldiers for an upcoming battle is confirmed by two facts: (1) David dispatched his general and senior officers for the census because they had the ability and training necessary to determine who was fit to be mustered into the military forces, and (2) the officers only counted men who were fit for military service.

WHAT WAS WRONG WITH THE CENSUS?

A publicly known census, especially one that lasted over nine months and involved senior military officers traveling through the entire Israelite nation, must have come to the attention of Israel's enemies, the nations that David was assembling forces to fight. Once the enemies learned the numbers of their opposing forces, including the areas from which they would be drafted, they could undertake preventative measures, with enormous negative consequences to the Israelites.

WHY WERE THE PEOPLE PUNISHED FOR DAVID'S MISDEED?

This question exists only if we are addressing a theological issue. Now that we know that David's wrong-headed act led to secret information being disseminated to the enemy forces, we understand that David himself caused the death of so many of his people.

---

19. Radak agrees that God did not cause David to count the Israelites of even suggest that he do so by prophecy.

WHAT DOES "DAVID'S HEART SMOTE HIM" MEAN?

The phrase "heart smote him" is a metaphor that has nothing at all to do with the heart. Whenever the heart is mentioned in Scripture, it refers to the mind, to thinking, for the ancients believed that thinking originates in the heart. Thus, the phrase means that David's thoughts bothered him, he was disturbed when reflecting on his actions.

DAVID'S CHOICE

It is now possible to interpret the subsequent events in the following way: David realized that he had made an enormous error, but he also understood that thinking about it or agonizing over it (repentance) would not help. It was too late. There was nothing he could do to help his people. The release of the secret information would result in the loss of many lives. Any actions he took could not change this fact. He chose to go ahead with the battle (which is not described in our text) and, so to speak, leave the decision up to God. This does not mean that God would interfere and determine the results of the battle. It means – as Maimonides states in 2:48 – that David and his men would fight as well as they could, and face the consequences.

The three options offered by the prophet Gad were, in fact, three possible natural outcomes of David's negligent behavior. His battle might have ended, as Gad predicted, in the Israelites fleeing from their enemies or in a famine like the one caused by Saul's war. David won his battle and there was no famine, but there were consequences to his misguided census. Quite possibly the third option, the plague, occurred because the great slaughter and the presence of dead bodies led to a plague that lasted three days. Alternatively, the seventy thousand men that were lost because of the "plague" were soldiers lost in battle, a far greater number than would have been lost if the census of his forces had not been publicized.

WHY WAS THE TRIBE OF JUDAH COUNTED SEPARATELY FROM THE OTHER TRIBES?

This leaves us with two unanswered questions. The first – why David counted the tribe of Judah separately – is very important to the understanding of early Israelite history. As we mentioned in chapter 22, the tribe of Judah was always treated differently, better, than the other Israelite tribes. This was one of the great mistakes made by Israelite leadership from the time of Joshua until the united tribes split during the reign of Solomon's son Rehoboam. During this entire period, Judah was always treated as a separate entity and given preferential treatment. This occurred over and over again, even after David and Solomon supposedly united the tribes into a single nation.

In 1 Kings 4:7–19, to cite a single example, Solomon is reported to have appointed twelve administrative officers over the land of Israel to provide food for him, conscript labor, and collect taxes. The twelve districts were generally not tribal territories and did not include the area assigned to the tribe of Judah, which was exempt from these requirements. As a result, the united tribes of Judah and Israel was in large part a domination of the tribes of Israel by the tribe of Judah. Thus it should surprise no one that the so-called unity government was unable to last very long and split when Solomon died.

PART 7
David's death

The first two chapters of the biblical book Kings serve as both a close of the life of King David, in essence the conclusion of the book Samuel, and an introduction to Kings, the assumption of the reign of David's son Solomon over the kingdom that David united.

David on His Death Bed

I KINGS 1

> While a cursory reading of chapter one may lead readers to think they understand what transpired, a closer look reveals that the chapter is quite opaque. I Chronicles 11–29 relates the history of King David. It leaves out much of his history, including David slaying Goliath and states that one of King David's warriors did so in I Chronicles 20:15.[1] It also deletes anything its author or editor felt demeaned David. Accordingly, chapters 1–2 are omitted, as well as his marriage to non-Israelites, and the tale of the two prostitutes in chapter 3. According to Chronicles, David was not senile at the end of his life and did not have to be tricked to arrange for Solomon to succeed him, and he spent much of his life and his final years helping Solomon, who he had long-wanted to be his successor, to build the temple.

WHAT HAPPENED IN I KINGS 1?

David was about seventy years old. He had served as king of Judah for some seven years and of the united tribes for about thirty-three years.[2] He was in bed suffering from cold. Attempts to warm him with clothing failed. His advisors suggested that placing a beautiful virgin in his bed would warm him.[3] They brought him Abishag, from the Israelite city Shunem. "But the king knew her not," he was unable to have sex with her.[4] Ehrlich notes the irony: the elderly senile king who "loved women

---

1. II Samuel 21:19 also states that someone other than David killed Goliath.
2. II Samuel 5:4.
3. In I Samuel 16:15 and 16, Saul's advisors suggest to him that he may overcome his depression if he brings in someone to play music for him. In Esther 2:2, Ahasuerus' advisors suggest that he find another beautiful woman to replace Vashti. In these two instances, as well as this one, the advice is necessary because the king himself is unable to act. Also, in all three, what follows causes problems for the king.
4. Verse 4. Why a virgin? David was not particular about this. He had married at least one

above all," as stated hyperbolically in 1 Samuel 1:27 that he loved Jonathan more than he loved women.[5] Ehrlich adds that Kings mentions Abishag for two reasons: to show that David was senile and as an introduction of her who will appear in chapter 2 as the woman Adonijah desires, to his peril.

Meanwhile, David's oldest living son Adonijah,[6] a very handsome lad[7] whom David loved, who had assumed, as others had, that he would succeed his father as king, had been acting as the successor for some time without his father reprimanding him.[8] He was David's oldest living son, and beside being allowed by David to do as he liked, he had the support to succeed his father by David's older leaders. Seeing that his father is in precipitous decline and from all appearances unable to function as king, Adonijah felt it was time to assume what he felt was his rightful role. Ehrlich understands that David wanted Adonijah to succeed him and only substituted Solomon because he was now senile and influenced by Nathan.

Adonijah conferred with David's commander Joab and one of David's two priests Abiathar who agreed that he had the right to be king and that now was a proper time to assume this role.[9] Adonijah gathered a princely escort of fifty

---

woman who was previously married. He took Saul's daughter Michal back as his wife after her father took her from him and married her to another man. Perhaps his advisors thought a virgin would excite him. Probably reflecting the science of his day, the fifteenth century, Abarbanel suggested that virgins give off more heat. ArtScroll argues that David was sexually capable but did not have sex with Abishag out of respect for Bat-sheba.

5. Ehrlich. *Mikra Kipheshuto*, 262.

6. The name means "God is my lord."

7. Should we see here a reminder that Samuel erred in choosing Saul as king because he looked good (1 Samuel 9:2), he was a head taller than other men; and he almost erred in choosing David's older brother because he was very handsome. We are also reminded that David himself is called handsome (1 Samuel 16:12), as well as David's son Absalom (II Samuel 14:25).

8. Verse 6 states: "and his father had not bothered him his entire life, saying, 'why are you doing this?'" By "doing this," we can assume that David meant, acting as the inheritor of my throne. Abarbanel interprets that David only allowed Adonijah to act in a princely manner, he had no idea that his son wanted to be king.

9. Regarding Abiathar, see 1 Samuel 22. There is no hint that this was a rebellion. Joab, for example, although hot-headed and precipitous in his actions, always had David's interests at heart. He and the others who joined Adonijah most likely saw how well David treated his eldest living son and thought that as the eldest, he should rule. In contrast, Rashi asserts that Joab feared that David would command his successor to kill him because he had killed Abner, Amasa, and Absalom, in II Samuel 3:27, 20:10, and 18:14, respectively, but was convinced that Adonijah would not do so. Similarly, Rashi states that Abiathar felt he would be deposed from the priesthood if Solomon became king.

men to run before him[10] and led a coronation ceremony with sacrifices of sheep, oxen, and fatlings, near a spring at En-rogel.[11] All of David's sons were invited except for Solomon.[12] He made the same error that he learned from his father, he ignored the northern tribes, and was also accompanied by "all the men of [the tribe of] Judah."[13] While he had a large entourage, Benaiah, Joab's brother and one of David's commanders, the other priest Zadok, Nathan the prophet,[14] David's "mighty men,"[15] and others did not join Adonijah.

Hearing of Adonijah's act and since he loved Solomon, the prophet Nathan approached Solomon's mother Bat-sheba, told her what Adonijah had done, and suggested that unless she could persuade her husband to appoint her son as king soon, Adonijah would succeed David. He suggested that she say that David had sworn to make Solomon king, and ask why does Adonijah reign? Ehrlich comments that it is clear that David never promised to make Solomon king; if he did swear so to Bat-sheba, she would have acted on her own without being pushed

---

10. Earlier, in II Samuel 15:1, Absalom wanted to make himself king and also had fifty men run before him. While it is clear that the escort was to show that he would be king, the significance of the fifty is obscure.

11. It was customary for the Davidic kings to be anointed near water. Solomon was also crowned near water. Some say that this was a symbol that the king's reign should flow smoothly like a spring or river (BabylonianTalmud, *Horiot* 12a). Others see the ceremony beside water as being part of a superstitious belief that God is found near water. See my discussion on this idea in my *Maimonides: The Exceptional Mind*, chapter 27. Maimonides states in *Mishneh Torah*, The Laws of Kings and their Wars, 1:11, "The kings of the Davidic dynasty must be anointed near a stream." He says in 1:10 that the Davidic kings are anointed with a special oil. In 1:12, he writes that a son who succeeds his father is not anointed unless there is controversy, in order to quell all disputes. "Therefore, they anointed Solomon, because Adonijah laid claim to the throne."

12. The chapter does not disclose why Solomon was not invited. It may be that Adonijah saw something in Solomon that caused him to think that Solomon either disliked him of that he wanted to be king. Perhaps also he saw that the prophet Nathan wanted Solomon to be king and wanted to do what he could to avoid Nathan's influence.

13. Verse 9. An obvious exaggeration (Abarbanel).

14. Nathan had special love for Solomon since his birth. In II Samuel 12:25, he called Solomon Jedidiah, which means "beloved of the Lord." No reason is given there for Nathan's love of Solomon or why if the prophet named him Jedidiah, he wasn't called by that name. Some scholars think that Jedidiah was his real name and Solomon was the name he assumed when he ascended the throne of his father. This is pure conjecture.

15. See the list of these men in II Samuel 23:8–39. It is possible that the "mighty men" did not join Adonijah because they followed Benaiah who was their commander. Why Benaiah did not join Adonijah with his brother Joab is unclear.

by Nathan to do so. Nathan added that he would also come to the king after her "and confirm your words."[16]

Bat-sheba was at this time elderly. Her husband David was seventy-years-old and she was likely near that age, which was old age during this era. We will encounter her again in the next chapter where she foolishly accepted Adonijah's request to be able to marry the virgin who lay with David, a clear violation of the practice of the time when the bedding of a king's wife or concubine indicated the seizure of his crown. Here she was passive until prompted by Nathan; she was being led, as was David, by Nathan's machinations.

Bat-sheba said what Nathan suggested and added that David did not seem to know what had transpired, Adonijah was engaged in a coronation ceremony, Solomon was not invited, David needed to make his selection of his successor known, and if Adonijah was made king he would kill her and Solomon.[17] Nathan did come after Bat-sheba spoke to David, but he did not confirm David's promise to Bat-sheba but that Adonijah had proclaimed himself king.[18]

David agreed that he swore to make Solomon king, although no such promise is contained in the Bible. David ordered Zadok the priest, Nathan the prophet, and his commander Benaiah to place Solomon on his mule,[19] bring him to the pool at Gihon, have Zadok and Nathan anoint Solomon as king, blow a shofar, proclaim Solomon king, bring him to the throne and sit him there. They did as David ordered. They were joined by David's personal bodyguards, the Cherethites

---

16. Verse 14.

17. It should not be assumed that Bat-sheba added these ideas on her own initiative. It is more likely that they were also suggested by Nathan. It is the customary practice throughout the Bible that when an incident is repeated everything is not mentioned during the first narration but is included when the narration is repeated.

18. Arguably, this makes sense, because how would Nathan know about a private conversation between spouses. Also, he may have refrained from mentioning it because he did not want to lie. However, on the other hand, he could reasonably know because Bat-sheba had told him about the conversation, and David would not have been bothered that Bat-sheba told him of his promise. Or he knew because he was a prophet.

19. The Babylonian Talmud *Sanhedrin* 22a states that since no commoner may ride on the king's mule, this would further impress the people that David wanted Solomon to be king. Ahasuerus was unconcerned about this matter; he had Mordecai ride on his horse. Ehrlich explains that until after the reign of King David the ancient Israelites preferred to ride on mules rather than horses, although they used horses for chariots. Even Absalom rode into battle on a mule (II Samuel 18:9).

and Pelethites. "And all the people came after him, and the people piped with pipes and with great joy, and the earth shook because of the noise."[20]

When Adonijah's assembly heard what had transpired, they dispersed. Adonijah became frightened, ran to the altar of God, and held on to the horns of the altar, which was considered a sanctuary, a place from which criminals could not be taken to be punished. He agreed to leave the altar when Solomon promised not to harm him as long as he acted properly. Then Solomon said to him, "Go to your house."[21]

DAVID'S MENTAL CONDITION

But, did the senile David really order the details of the coronation? And in chapter 2, did he give Solomon instructions? Or, were the recitation of these acts the additions of an editor?

Commentators disagree concerning David's mental health in this episode during these last days of his life. Ehrlich, J. Robinson, and many others, contend that David was senile at this time. Slotki writes that the statement in verse 4 that David "knew her [the virgin] not," may "serve the purpose of indicating the wane of David's physical faculties accompanied by the weakening also of his mind and will-power, as shown in this chapter by the ease with which he was influenced by those around him."[22] Cogan refers to this verse as well as verse 18 where David did not know that Adonijah was proclaiming himself king, that the remarks "confirm the decrepit state of David's old age…. "David's unawareness."[23] He had never promised Bat-sheba that Solomon would succeed him. The alleged promise is not mentioned anywhere in the Bible. David treated Adonijah as his successor, as seemingly shown in verse 6.

Ehrlich compares the senile David with the patriarch Jacob. Both were active tricksters in their youth and were themselves tricked in their old age when they acted passively. Jacob tricked his father Isaac and stole the blessing intended for his brother Esau. Later his sons lied to him saying Joseph was dead, and as a result

---

20. Verse 40, hyperbole.
21. It is unclear whether these words in verse 53 reflect Solomon's unconditional pardon or a command not to engage in the future in any public affairs.
22. I.W. Slotki, *Kings* (London: The Soncino Press, 1961), 2.
23. Mordechai Cogan, *1 Kings*, The Anchor Yale Bible (Yale University Press, 2001), 156.

he mourned for his most beloved son for some twenty years. David, according to Ehrlich, lied to his wife Michal and her brother Jonathan that he loved them, now his wife lied to him that he swore to make Solomon king. Being senile, or close to it, he, like Jacob before him, believed what he heard. Robinson contrasts David with Moses who "at the end of Deuteronomy is said to have kept all his powers and faculties, and therefore his capacity to exercise authority, until his death."[24]

Of course, one can reasonably argue that even senile people can have moments of clarity. However, chapter 2 verse 3 seems to override this interpretation. It states that King David advised his son Solomon: "keep the charge of the Lord your God: walk in his ways, keep his statutes, commandments, ordinances, and testimonies, as written in the laws of Moses, so that you can succeed in all that you do, and wherever you turn."

The problem with these words is that they seem to have been added by an editor, which suggests that the end of chapter one was similarly added by an editor. The additions in chapter one were most likely inserted to show that Solomon did not attain his kingship solely by deceit: David wanted him to serve as his successor and even ordered how the coronation would take place. The addition in chapter two was added to show that Solomon did not act against Joab, Shimei, and his brother out of malice; and to remove any moral and legal blame upon Solomon for killing Joab and Shimei. Solomon was fulfilling his father's will; the wise king David suggested that he kill them.[25] The editorial additions were also probably inserted as an attempt to remind readers that God only favors people who obey the divine law.

Why does 2:3 seem to indicate that it is a late scribal addition? It speaks about the law (*Torah*) of Moses. We saw in our analysis of Joshua, Judges, and Samuel more than several dozen examples showing that the Israelites during these periods knew nothing about the Torah of Moses, and the people and their leaders acted contrary to what is mandated in the Torah. In our earlier book about David, we saw the same. It is not until the kingship of Josiah that the Torah is mentioned.[26] So its

---

24. J.R. Robinson, *The First Book of Kings*, The Cambridge Bible Commentary, 1972, 24.
25. Needless to say, the attempt to place the blame upon David fails because one cannot justify immoral behavior by saying I was ordered to commit murder, as Adolf Eichmann claimed.
26. It is only mentioned in Joshua 1:7–9 and II Kings 14:6 before the time of Josiah in II Kings 22. These two earlier mentions may also be late editorial additions.

uncharacteristic mention here raises the idea that verse 3 is a late addition. Ehrlich points out that the editorial addition must have been added after the completion of the biblical book Chronicles because the clause about Moses' Torah, which fits in with Chronicles' methodology, is absent in 1 Chronicles 26:24.

In contrast, people such as Abarbanel insist that while David was physically frail, his mind continued to function properly, and even in his frail condition he acted decisively for the benefit of his people by insisting that Solomon be king. Radak states that his physical condition was frail due to his constant battles to secure his country, but his mind was clear.

WHY WAS DAVID COLD?

The Babylonian Talmud *Berachot* 62b contends sermonically that clothing did not warm David because God punished him for not treating clothing properly. In 1 Samuel 24:5, when he encountered Saul, he tore Saul's clothing when the king was asleep to show him that he had the opportunity to kill him but did not do so. Rashi states that after David counted the Israelites in a census and saw the many deaths that resulted from the census, he chilled and was never warm thereafter. This idea is not in scripture.

BAT-SHEBA

From the time of Bat-sheba's loss of her first child, the child of David, until now, there is no mention of Bat-sheba. If David had continued to have good relations with his wife, there was no reason for him to try to bed a virgin. We can assume that Bat-sheba was now elderly, but even an elderly woman is warm. Apparently, soon after he bedded her, David's relationship with her cooled. So many deaths resulted from David's behavior with Bat-sheba, but his feelings and need for her may have ceased.

THE CORONATION CEREMONIES

Ceremonies are important to people, especially for events such as the installation of a king and the inauguration of a president.[27] Frequently, old practices are used to connect the present event with those in the past. This accounts for the use of the anointing with oil, which according to tradition was prepared by Moses and

---

27. As well as events such as marriage.

used only on special occasions. It accounts also for the blasting of the shofar, used also by Absalom in II Samuel 15:10 when he wanted people to recognize that he was the new king. We can safely assume that the shofar was the anciently-used ram's horn rather than a metal trumpet, just as the ram's horn is still used today during the holiday of Rosh Hashanah rather than a trumpet.[28]

SUMMARY

Solomon became king because he was one of David's sons; not the son most successful in battle, but the son most successful in palace intrigue.[29]

---

28. Similarly, candles are lit before the Sabbath rather than electric light, although both fulfil the law, because candles were used in the past.
29. Robinson, *The First Book of Kings*, 20.

David's Final Instructions
to Solomon

I KINGS 2

Solomon was now installed as king. David gave his son final instructions before his death. These instructions, while practical and common in ancient times, are immoral and contrary to the Torah. It is as if neither David nor Solomon knew that people should not be killed without a trial. David told Solomon that he was unable to kill certain men during his lifetime, although they deserved to be killed. For political reasons, because his murder of these men would make other men who liked the murdered men angry at him and rebel, he instructed Solomon to "be a man,"[30] and use his mind to find a way to kill them. Soon, Solomon found a reason and killed them. In essence, this is arguably the first example of the famed "wise Solomon" showing his wisdom. But is it?

DAVID'S REQUEST OF SOLOMON

David reminded his son that his commander Joab killed Abner[31] and Amasa,[32] two commanders of opposing forces who had agreed to join David. He did not mention Joab's murder of David's son Absalom.[33] Apparently, although greatly bothered by this murder, he focused on the two murders that had the potential of causing a rebellion.

---

30. The word for "man" in verse 2 is *ish*, which the rabbis generally understood to denote a better than usual man, as in *Ethics of the Fathers* 2:6, "where there are no men, strive to be a man." Since David is requesting Solomon to commit murder, this is ironic.

31. II Samuel 3:27ff.

32. II Samuel 20:8ff.

33. II Samuel 18:14f and 19:6ff.

Although contrary to the biblical requirement to have a trial, David advised his son to "do [to him] according to your wisdom,"[34] "you are a wise man and will know what to do to him," meaning, find some plausible pretext to kill him.

In contrast, David requested Solomon to reward the sons of Barzillai[35] for aiding him when he fled Jerusalem to avoid Absalom's rebellious attack.[36] He did not request Solomon to take care of Saul's son Jonathan's descendants, even though he swore to Jonathan that he would take care of them, possibly because Jonathan's descendants might prompt the northern tribes, to which they belonged, to rebel.

Returning to the subject of revenge, David requested Solomon to avenge the grievous curse that Shimei the Benjamite placed upon him when he fled from Absalom[37] by killing him, even though he swore to Shimei that he would not harm him. As with his oath to Jonathan, David ignored what he swore to do in violation of the Decalogue's mandate not to swear falsely.

The two acts of revenge, although contrary to the Torah and our current understanding of morality, fit in with the practices of the time for kings to take brutal actions against those who oppose them.

Another ancient practice was that when a man became king he removed any possible future threat. This included Adonijah, Solomon's older brother who had claimed and would claim again that he had the right to succeed their father. It also left the priest Abiathar who had joined Adonijah when he attempted to seize the crown.[38] Although unmentioned by David, who was seemingly focusing on his own hurts, Solomon addressed this possible future problem.

ADONIJAH

While Solomon acted cunningly, Adonijah made a foolish mistake. Forgetting that the ancients felt that bedding the wife or concubine of the present or prior

---

34. Verse 6.

35. Verse 7.

36. II Samuel 17:27ff and 19:33ff. David's mention of Barzillai's action of helping him during Absalom's rebellion, while speaking of Joab's murders, and before he continued with the subject of revenge, against Shimei, suggests that that despite no explicit mention of revenge against Joab for killing Absalom, it was on his mind.

37. II Samuel 16:5ff.

38. I Kings 1:5ff. In verse 15 of this chapter, Adonijah tells Bat-sheba, "You know that the kingdom was intended for me, and that all of Israel looked to me to reign."

king was a symbolic act showing that the person doing it was assuming the reign of the kingdom,[39] Adonijah approached Bat-sheba and requested her to go to her son Solomon and request that he allow Adonijah to marry Abishag, the woman who joined David in bed to keep him warm.[40] Bat-sheba agreed to his request, but Solomon saw it as a threat to his rule and had Adonijah killed.[41]

ABIATHAR

Solomon did not kill the priest Abiathar who had joined Adonijah in the ceremony in which Adonijah proclaimed himself king, presumably because he was a priest and feared the displeasure of the people. Solomon told Abiathar that he deserved death and banished him.

JOAB

When Joab heard what happened to Adonijah and Abiathar, he realized he was next since he also participated in the crowning ceremony of Adonijah as well as killing three men against the wishes of King David. He ran to the Tent of the Lord and grasped the horns of the altar believing it gave him sanctuary. He overlooked or, more likely, did not know that Exodus 21:12–14 states that if one murders a person willingly, he may be executed even if he seeks sanctuary by holding on to the altar. Solomon ordered Benaiah, one of Solomon's commanders, to go to the Tent of the Lord and kill him there. Again, contrary to the Torah, there was no trial.

SHIMEI

Solomon apparently could think of no ruse as an excuse to execute Shimei. True,

---

39. Compare II Samuel 3:7–8, 16:21.

40. It is possible that Adonijah made his request to Solomon through Bat-sheba because he felt that she would be able to influence her son, or because he felt she was not to bright and would not recall the symbolism of bedding the king's woman. There is some support for the view that Bat-sheba was not too bright. Although she obviously wanted her son to be king, she needed the prophet Nathan to urge her to go to the king and to tell her what to say. Additionally, she did not think that what Adonijah requested was wrong. Should we suppose that showing Solomon's mother being foolish is an ironic reflection on her son? Alternatively, is it possible that she knew what she was doing and accepted Adonijah's request knowing it would result in Adonijah's death and the removal of a possible upcoming threat to her son?

41. The text does not allow us to determine if Adonijah wanted Abishag as a consolation prize, a symbol that he was the expected and future king, or he was simply in love with the beautiful woman.

the people knew that Shimei cursed King David, but this was long ago and David did not punish him for his act, and had even sworn that he would not harm him.[42] So, Solomon sentenced him to leave his home and dwell in Jerusalem. He warned Shimei that if he leaves Jerusalem he would be in disobedience of the king and would be killed.[43]

This is what happened. Three years later,[44] two of Shimei's servants ran away, Shimei followed them from Jerusalem to the Philistine city of Gat and brought them back, and Solomon ordered Benaiah to kill him, again without a trial.

The chapter ends "So the kingdom was established in Solomon's hand," meaning he had now delivered himself from all internal threats. Or so he thought.

DOES THIS CHAPTER SHOW SOLOMON ACTED WISELY?

Solomon is fabled as a wise king. He killed Joab, Shimei, and Adonijah. Are these acts, which are contrary to the Torah and basic morality, the behavior of a wise man, or are they the cunning guile of a brutal king?

---

42. II Samuel 16:5–13 and 19:16–24.

43. It seems that Solomon wanted Shimei where he could keep an eye on him and, more importantly, confine him in such a way that Shimei would at some time leave the city thinking he was safe, and Solomon would then have the excuse he needed to kill him.

44. The ubiquitous "three" again, a typical biblical topos and does not indicate an exact period of time.

Afterword

This study shows that the great and highly respected King David was not what people think, nor what they hear about him from pulpits and learn in school. David was human. He made mistakes. We also saw that while the book of Samuel is considered a holy book and part of the Bible, like the other post-Pentateuchal books until the time of King Josiah, the people in these books performed many acts that are contrary to the mandates of the Torah.

DAVID'S MISTAKES

David made many mistakes as king. Three mistakes that he made had substantial consequences that affected the lives of many people.

David bedding Bat-sheba and murdering her husband together with the troops that were with him resulted in a series of terrible events and many deaths: the death of his and Bat-sheba's first born child, his son Amnon following in his father's footsteps by raping his half-sister, David failing to take action and punish Amnon, Absalom taking revenge by killing Amnon, David not punishing Absalom but showing him no love, Absalom's anger, Absalom's revenge against his father by starting a rebellion resulting in David needing (or feeling the need) to retreat from Jerusalem, a war followed in which there were 20,000 deaths and the death of Absalom, and Absalom's death had a devastating impact upon David

David's second most consequential mistake was his repeated mistreatments of the northern tribes. True, there were tensions between Judah and the other tribes since the days of Joshua, if not before. He knew he had to gain the trust of the ten tribes and secure their allegiance. He did so by moving his capital from Hebron in the land of Judah and placing it in Jerusalem which was located between Judah and the ten tribes. Yet, he did not remain sufficiently sensitive to their feelings. He allowed the Gibeonites to kill seven of King Saul's sons. He insulted Saul's grandson, the son of Saul's son Jonathan, by not rejecting the slander by Ziba against the grandson, and gave Ziba half of Saul's property. He did not allow the men of the northern tribes to accompany his train when he returned to Jerusalem after Absalom's rebellion, ignored their complaint and let overzealous leaders of the tribe of Judah mistreat them, and more.

David's third most grievous error, again the result of a failure to think before he acted, is his public census of his people to determine what forces were available for war, resulting in the enemy knowing that he was preparing to attack them, their preparation for the assault, and the loss of some 70,000 men of David's army.

WHERE II SAMUEL SEEMS TO INDICATE THAT THE AUTHOR DID NOT KNOW ABOUT THE TORAH

Scholars contend that there are many indications in the book of Samuel that the book's author knew nothing about Moses's Torah, and may not have known about the biblical books of Joshua and Judges. I identified thirty-nine such indications in my two prior books about Samuel and David. There are an additional eighteen in this volume, fifty-seven in all.

1. Deuteronomy 24:4 forbids a man who divorced his wife to remarry her if after the divorce she married another man, yet David did so in chapter 3.
2. II Samuel 6 ignores the law in Numbers 3:31 that the ark may only be transported by priests carrying it by its poles. David had it carried on a wagon.
3. Like Samuel before him in I Samuel 2:18, although not a priest, David garbed himself in the priestly ephod when he danced "before the Lord with all his might" in 6:14.[45]
4. In chapter 8, David fought and killed Moabites ignoring the prohibition to do so in Deuteronomy 2:9.
5. In 8:18, David made his sons priests despite Exodus 28:1 stating that only the descendant of Moses' brother Aaron are allowed to serve as priests.
6. David cut the sinews of hind legs of hundreds of horses in chapter 8 apparently so that they could not be used in chariots in war against Israel. This is contrary to the Torah rule forbidding harming animals in Deuteronomy 20:19.

---

45. The ephod is not mentioned in Exodus 28:40 as a dress of an ordinary priest, only the high priest, but during the days of Samuel it was considered the dress of a priest.

7. David murdered two-thirds of the defeated Moabites in chapter 8 despite Deuteronomy 2:9 prohibiting "Do not engage in war with them." These were captured prisoners. The text is unclear if the persons killed included women and children.

8. David committed adultery in chapter 11 with the wife of Uriah in violation of the prohibition in the Decalogue in Exodus 20:14 and Deuteronomy 5:18.

9. David caused the murder of Uriah and others in the same chapter, although forbidden in the Decalogue in Exodus 20:13 and Deuteronomy 5:17.

10. Verse 13:13 seems to say that a man may marry his half-sister, while Leviticus 18:9 forbids such a marriage.

11. David did not require Amnon to marry Tamar, the woman he raped, as required by Deuteronomy 22:28, 29.

12. David arranged for Saul's innocent children to be killed in chapter 21.

13. Chapter 21 seems to indicate that Saul killed innocent Gibeonites despite Joshua's promise in Joshua 9:15ff that they would not be harmed.

14. David allowed the bodies of Saul's executed children to hang for months contrary to Deuteronomy 21:23.

15. The text does not indicate that Saul's children were guilty of any wrong, yet David had them killed for their father's misdeed, a violation of Deuteronomy 24:16.

16. David advised his son Solomon in 1 Kings 1 to kill Joab and Shimei contrary to the Torah which demands that one not be sentenced to death without a trial and at least two witnesses to the crime.

17. Solomon killed Adonijah in 1 Kings 2 without a trial and witnesses.

18. Despite the Decalogue mandating that God's name should not be taken in vain, meaning do not swear falsely, David violated his oaths both to Saul's son Jonathan that he would protect his descendants by ignoring his son for a decade, not telling Solomon to protect the son's descendants, and violated his oath to Shimei to whom he swore not to harm him when he told Solomon to find a way to kill him.

DO WE HAVE NON-BIBLICAL PROOF THAT DAVID ACTUALLY LIVED?

The Biblical Archaeology Society answers that the only proof that some scholars think proves the existence of David is the Tel Dan inscription on a stone slab that was written in the ninth-century BCE which was discovered in 1993 in northern Israel.

The fragmentary inscription commemorates the victory of an Aramean king over his two southern neighbors: the "king of Israel" and the "king of the House of David." The king boasts that he defeated several thousand Israelite and Judahite horsemen and charioteers. The fragments do not preserve the names of the kings involved in this battle. Most, but not all scholars believe the stela recounts a campaign of Hazael of Damascus in which he defeated both Jehoram of Israel and Ahaziah of Judah.

The "House of David" inscription has its skeptics, especially the so-called biblical minimalists, who dismiss the "House of David" reading as implausible and even sensationalistic. "In a famous BAR [Biblical Archaeology Review magazine] article, Philip Davies argued that the Hebrew term *bytdwd* referred to a specific place (akin to *bytlhm* for Bethlehem) rather than the ancestral dynasty of David." Most biblical "scholars and archaeologists rejected Davies' skepticism and accepted that the Tel Dan stela had supplied the first concrete proof of a historical King David from the Bible, making it one of the top Biblical archaeology discoveries reported in BAR."

THE GOAL OF THE TORAH

The majority of people, even non-religious people – Jews, Christians, Moslems, and others – think that the Hebrew Bible was composed to teach spirituality and holiness. Yet we see that the Torah's depiction of David is on the whole negative; it points out the errors of the king.

This situation is not unique. The Hebrew Bible depicts the mistakes of virtually all the people described in it.[46]

We need a new understanding. The writers of the Hebrew Bible did not want to teach spirituality. They wanted to tell their people the history of their ancestors as they understood the history. Their message was "learn from their faults."

---

46. Such as Abraham not telling the whole truth when he said Sarah was his sister and when Jacob stole the blessing intended for Esau from their father Isaac.

Sources

Abarbanel, Isaac. *Perush Abarbanel* (Abarbanel's commentary). New York: Seforim Torah Vodaath, 1955.

Abramski, Samuel, ed. *Samuel.* Olam Hatanakh. Jerusalem: Divrei Hayamim, 2002.

Babylonian Talmud: *Avoda Zara, Baba Metziah, Berakhot, Horiot, Kiddushin, Megilah, Seder Mo'ed, Mo'ed Kattan, Sanhedrin, Shabbat, Sota, Sukkah, Yevamot, Yoma.*

Bar-Eitan, Zev. *Abravanel's World of Torah.* Renaissance Torah Press, 2016.

ben Gershom, Levi (Gersonides). *Peirushei Ralbag Nevi'im Rishonim* (Gersonides' commentary on the Early Prophets). Jerusalem: Mossad HaRav Kook, 2008.

Buttrick, George A. *The Interpreter's Bible.* New York: Abingdon, 1957.

Cogan, Mordechai, *1 Kings,* The Anchor Yale Bible, Yale University Press, 2001.

Drazin, Israel. *Joshua.* Unusual Bible Interpretations. Jerusalem: Gefen Publishing House, 2014.

———. *Maimonides and the Biblical Prophets.* Jerusalem: Gefen Publishing House, 2009.

———. *Maimonides: The Exceptional Mind.* Jerusalem: Gefen Publishing House, 2008.

———. *Mysteries of Judaism.* Jerusalem: Gefen Publishing House, 2014.

———. *Mysteries of Judaism II: How the Rabbis and Others Changed Judaism.* Jerusalem: Gefen Publishing House, 2017.

———. *Ruth, Esther, and Judith.* Unusual Bible Interpretations. Jerusalem: Gefen Publishing House, 2016.

———. *Who Really Was the Biblical David?* Jerusalem: Gefen Publishing House, 2017.

Driver, S.R. *Introduction to the Literature of the Old Testament.* International Theological Library. T. & T. Clark, 1891.

Ehrlich, Arnold Bogomil. *Mikra Kipheshuto* (The Bible according to its literal meaning). Ed. Harry M. Orlinsky. New York: Ktav Publishing House, 1901, 1969.

Epstein, Baruch. *Tosaphot Berakhah*. Moreshet Publishing House, 1999.

———. *Mekor Barukh*. Lithuania, Rom, 1928.

Even-Shoshan, Avraham ed. *A New Concordance of the Old Testament* (Kiryat-Sefer, 1989).

———. *Tosaphot Berakhah*, Moreshet Publishing House, 1999.

Goldman, S. *Samuel*. London: The Soncino Press, 1951.

Herring, B. *Caspi's Gevia Kesef*. Ktav Publishing House, 1982.

Hertzberg, Hans Wilheim. *I & II Samuel*. The Old Testament Library, 1964.

Hirsch, S.R. *The Pentateuch*. New York: Judaica Press, 1971.

Hoenig, Sidney B. and Samuel H. Rosenberg, *A Guide to the Prophets*, Yeshiva University, 1942

Holy Scriptures According to the Masoretic Text. Philadelphia: The Jewish Publication Society of America, 1960.

Josephus, Flavius. *The Antiquities of the Jews*. Trans. William Whiston. Nashville, T.N.: Thomas Nelson, 2003. First published 1737.

Kaufmann, Yehezkel. *A Biblical Account of the Conquest of Canaan*. Jerusalem: The Hebrew University Magnes Press, 1985.

Kennedy, Archibald Robert Sterling. *Samuel* (T.C. & E.C. Clarke, 1905).

Kiel, Yehuda. *Samuel*. 2 vols. Daat Mikra. Jerusalem: Mossad HaRav Kook, 1981.

Kirschenbaum, Aaron. *Self-Incrimination in Jewish Law*. New York: Burning Bush Press, 1970.

Maimonides, Moses. *Guide of the Perplexed*. Hebrew translation: Alharizi, Ibn Tibbon with Hanarboni. New York: 1946. English translation: M. Friedlander. New York: Dover, 1956.

———. *Maimonides: The Commandments*. Trans. C.B. Chavel. London: The Soncino Press, 1967.

———. *Mishneh Torah*. Ed. Shabse Frankel. Jerusalem: Hotza'at Shabse Frankel, 1975. First published 1180.

McCarter, P. Kyle, Jr. *I Samuel*. The Anchor Bible. New York: Doubleday, 1980.

Midrash: *Genesis Rabba, Numbers Rabba, Sifrei, Seder Olam, Midrash Shmuel, Midrash Ruth Rabba, Midrash Pirkei d'Rabbi Eliezer*

Mishnah: *Avot.*

Plato. *Symposium.*

Robinson, J.R. *The First Book of Kings,* The Cambridge Bible Commentary, 1972.

Samuel. Olam Hatanakh. Jerusalem: Divrei Hayamim, 2002.

Scholem, Gershom. *Encyclopedia Judaica,* vol. 3. Jerusalem: Keter, 1972.

Scripture: Genesis, Exodus, Leviticus, Numbers, Deuteronomy, Joshua, Judges, Samuel, Kings, Isaiah, Jeremiah, Ezekiel, Hosea, Amos, Jonah, Habakkuk, Zechariah, Malachi, Psalms, Job, Ruth, Lamentations, Esther, Ezra, Nehemiah, Chronicles, Ecclesiasticus, Second Corinthians

Segal, M.T. *Mavoi Hamikra* (Introduction to the Bible). Jerusalem: Kiryat Sefer, 1977.

Slotki, I.W. *Kings.* London: The Soncino Press, 1961.

Smith, H.P. *A Critical and Exegetical Commentary on the Book of Samuel.* International Critical Commentary, Edinburgh: Clark, 1899.

Index

About the Author

DR. ISRAEL DRAZIN

EDUCATION: Dr. Drazin, born in 1935, received three rabbinical degrees in 1957, a B.A. in Theology in 1957, an M.Ed. In Psychology in 1966, a JD in Law in 1974, a M.A. in Hebrew Literature in 1978 and a Ph.D. with honors in Aramaic Literature in 1981. Thereafter, he completed two years of post-graduate study in both Philosophy and Mysticism and graduated the U.S. Army's Command and General Staff College and its War College for generals in 1985.

MILITARY: Brigadier General Drazin entered Army Active Duty, at age 21, as the youngest U.S. Chaplain ever to serve on active duty. He served on active duty from 1957 to 1960 in Louisiana and Germany, and then joined the active reserves and soldiered, in increasing grades, with half a dozen units. From 1978 until 1981, he lectured at the US Army Chaplains School on legal subjects. In March 1981, the Army requested that he take leave from civil service and return to active duty to handle special constitutional issues. He was responsible for preparing the defense in the trial challenging the constitutionality of the Army Chaplaincy; the military chaplaincies of all the uniformed services, active and reserve, as well as the Veteran's Administration, were attacked utilizing a constitutional rationale and could have been disbanded. The Government won the action in 1984 and Drazin was awarded the prestigious *Legion of Merit*. "Awarded for exceptionally meritorious conduct in the performance of outstanding services to the United States." This award is only one of two awards that can be worn around one's neck; the other is the Medal of Honor. Drazin returned to civilian life and the active reserves in 1984 as Assistant Chief of Chaplains, the highest reserve officer position available in the Army Chaplaincy, with the rank of Brigadier General. He was the first Jewish person to serve in this capacity in the U.S. Army. During his military career, he revolutionized the role of military chaplains making them officers responsible for the free exercise rights of all military personnel; requiring them to provide for the needs of people of all faiths as well as atheists. General Drazin completed this four-year tour of duty with honors in March 1988, culminating a total of 31 years of military duty.

ATTORNEY: Israel Drazin graduated from law school in 1974 and immediately began a private practice. He handled virtually all manners of suits; including, domestic, criminal, bankruptcy, accident and contract cases. He joined with his son in 1993 and formed offices in Columbia and Dundalk, Maryland. Dr. Drazin stopped actively practicing law in 1997, after 23 years, and became "Of Counsel" to the Law Offices of Drazin and Drazin, P.A.

CIVIL SERVICE: Israel Drazin joined the U.S. Civil Service in 1962 and remained a civil service employee, with occasional leave for military duty, until retirement in 1990. At retirement he accumulated 31 years of creditable service. During his U.S. Civil Service career, he held many positions; including, being an Equal Opportunity Consultant in the 1960s (advising insurance company top executives regarding civil rights and equal employment) and the head of Medicare's Civil Litigation Staff (supervising a team of lawyers who handled suits filed by and against the government's Medicare program). He also served as the director for all Maryland's Federal Agencies' relationship with the United Fund.

RABBI: Dr. Drazin was ordained as a rabbi in 1957 at Ner Israel Rabbinical College in Baltimore, Maryland and subsequently received semichot from two other rabbis. He entered on Army active duty in 1957. He left active duty in 1960 and officiated as a weekend rabbi at several synagogues, including being the first rabbi in Columbia, Maryland. He continued the uninterrupted weekend rabbinical practice until 1974 and then officiated as a rabbi on an intermittent basis until 1987. His rabbinical career totaled 30 years.

PHILANTHROPY: Dr. Drazin served as the Executive Director of the Jim Joseph Foundation, a charitable foundation that gives money to support Jewish education, for just over four years, from September 2000 to November 2004.

AUTHOR: Israel Drazin is the author of thirty-seven books, more than 500 popular and scholarly articles, and over 4,300 book and movie reviews. He wrote a book about the case he handled for the US Army, edited a book on legends, children's books, and scholarly books on the philosopher Maimonides and on the Aramaic translation of the Bible. His website is www.booksnthoughts.com. He places two essays on this site weekly as well as on his blog on Times of Israel.

LECTURES: Dr. Drazin delivered lectures at Howard Community College, Lynn University, and the US Army Chaplains School.

MEMBERSHIPS AND AWARDS: Brigadier General Drazin is admitted to practice law in Maryland, the Federal Court, and before the U.S. Supreme Court. He is a member of several attorney Bar Associations and the Rabbinical Council of America. He was honored with a number of military awards, the RCA 1985 Joseph Hoenig Memorial Award, and the Jewish Welfare Board 1986 Distinguished Service Award. Mayor Kurt Schmoke, of Baltimore, Maryland, named February 8, 1988 "Israel Drazin Day." A leading Baltimore Synagogue named him "Man of the Year" in 1990. He is included in the recent editions of *Who's Who in World Jewry*, *Who's Who in American Law*, *Who's Who in Biblical Studies and Archaeology*, and other *Who's Who* volumes.